John Crowe Ransom
and Allen Tate

John Crowe Ransom and Allen Tate

At Odds About the Ends of History and the Mystery of Nature

by MARION MONTGOMERY

McFarland & Company, Inc., Publishers
Jefferson, North Carolina, and London

LIBRARY OF CONGRESS CATALOGUING-IN-PUBLICATION DATA

Montgomery, Marion.
  John Crowe Ransom and Allen Tate : at odds about the ends of
history and the mystery of nature / by Marion Montgomery.
     p.   cm.
  Includes index.

  ISBN 0-7864-1435-9 (softcover : 50# alkaline paper)

  1. Ransom, John Crow, 1888–1974—Criticism and interpretation.
2. Tate, Allen, 1899– —Criticism and interpretation.   3. Ransom,
John Crowe, 1888–1974—Philosophy.   4. Southern States—
Intellectual life—1865–   5. Literature and history—Southern States.
6. Tate, Allen, 1899– —Philosophy.   7. Southern States—In
literature.   8. Agrarians (Group of writers)   9. Philosophy in
literature.   10. Nature in literature.   11. Fugitives (Group)
I. Title.
PS3535.A635Z785 2003
810.9'975—dc21
                                                      2003001314

British Library cataloguing data are available

©2003 Marion Montgomery. All rights reserved

*No part of this book may be reproduced or transmitted in any form
or by any means, electronic or mechanical, including photocopying
or recording, or by any information storage and retrieval system,
without permission in writing from the publisher.*

On the cover: Ransom (left) and Tate at Kenyon College, 1949
  (Kenyon College)

Manufactured in the United States of America

McFarland & Company, Inc., Publishers
  Box 611, Jefferson, North Carolina 28640
    www.mcfarlandpub.com

To the memory of Cleanth Brooks
and
In thanksgiving for Michael and Lindy Jordan

Contents

Preface   11

I. The Setting Forth   17

II. Of Children and Kittens   26

III. Getting at the Truth: The Nature of Intellect in Act   33

IV. The Mystery of Nature and the Brooding Breast of Love   43

V. Of Natural Rights and Natural Law: A Speculative Beginning   50

VI. The Problem of Getting to Know *Natural Rights* from *Natural Law*   58

VII. Concerning the Impieties of Aberrant Will   66

VIII. Loving the South, at a Growing Distance   74

IX. The Specialization of Applied Prosody   90

X. Angelism and the Poet's Made World   100

CONTENTS

XI. Ownership vs. Stewardship: Signposts
at the Parting of Ways   111

XII. The "Cranky" Distinction Between
Poetry and Religion   122

Afterword   137

Notes   143

Index   149

Mother Nature: "Take one giant step."
Human Nature: "Mother, may I?"
   —from *The Game of Natural Rights:*
    A Passion Play in Progress

"I think that the road is nature, with all the events and ventures we meet with on the way, and that the clear stream bearing all along is *grace*, which runs all along nature and makes of all events and ventures divine opportunities."
   —Jacques Maritain to Allen Tate,
    November 18, 1949

"I lead my own life better on this quiet Hill at Gambier, where I am in good company and pay almost no attention to the plains below."
   —John Crowe Ransom to Marion
    Montgomery, September 28, 1965

Preface

The pages that follow are a sort of completion of a breakfast at the University of Dallas nearly twenty years ago. That is, they are representative of what I trust is a growth in my understanding of central issues in literature and philosophy which I did not possess at that breakfast. As such, they serve as a tribute following my kind inclusion at that breakfast by two distinguished men of letters. The general occasion was a gathering of the literary contingent of the Fugitive-Agrarians. Andrew Lytle was in attendance at the conference as were Robert Penn Warren, Allen Tate and John Crowe Ransom. Donald Davidson, because of poor health, could not at the last minute attend, though he sent warm messages. The breakfast found me in company with Mr. Ransom and Mr. Tate, by appointment.

I was invited by these kind gentlemen to meet them. We lingered over coffee, talking for some time before the formal gatherings got under way that morning. I knew something of the excitement Dante describes as his own when in Limbo, under the guidance of Virgil, he joins the five greatest poets of antiquity, finding himself a "sixth amid such intelligences." The analogy is not, of course, quite appropriate, certainly not in a comparison of my presence to Dante's, but the sense of being included which he describes in his great poem is rather certainly much like my own on the breakfast occasion.

I was there, largely, because of a critique I had published of John Stewart's unsatisfactory study of the Fugitive-Agrarians, *The Burden of Time*. Stewart's capacity to deal with a central issue to the Fugitive-

Agrarians, and one I engage in the following pages, was insufficient, alas, and his book is seriously flawed in consequence. Mr. Tate was at the time of my essay (the Fall of 1966) teaching at the University of North Carolina at Greensboro. A student there had passed on my essay to him, and he wrote me with such enthusiasm as could but have pleased me, a beginning pilgrim on the road he and others had taken. He was particularly pleased at my having "rescued Donald Davidson from his obloquy" in my piece. As for my treatment of Mr. Ransom, "Your Aristotelean analysis of John Ransom's 'Bells for John Whiteside's Daughter' is, I am sure, the finest criticism that or any other poem of his has ever had." Given Mr. Tate's standing as poet and critic, it was high praise indeed, to say nothing of dangerous to its recipient. At any rate, it was that essay on Stewart's book that occasioned my inclusion at the breakfast, which I remember vividly, but in no explicit detail. For I am no Dante.

I do remember that Mr. Ransom knew of my piece, though I do not know that he had been as excited by it as was Mr. Tate. But then, it was not his nature to become overly excited. Mr. Tate could, I knew, commit himself strongly in matters literary. On one famous occasion, the awarding of the 1948 Bollingen Prize to Ezra Pound for his *Pisan Cantos*, he did so impressively. The twelve-member committee for the award included Tate, and other such notables as Eliot, Aiken, Auden, Warren, Robert Lowell, and Katherine Anne Porter. It included also Karl Shapiro, who raised public objection to the committee's decision, leading to controversial, heated arguments in the *Partisan Review*, extending into 1949 and in some degree still at issue. Tate took exception to William Barrett's attacks on the committee, saying, "I consider antisemitism [the charge Shapiro, and Barrett as editor of the *Partisan Review*, had raised against the committee] to be both cowardly and dishonorable." Barrett's argument accused the committee of bowing to Pound and his poem through their cowardliness. "I hope," Tate concluded, "that persons who wish to accuse me of cowardice and dishonor will do so henceforth personally, in my presence, so that I may dispose of the charge at some other level than that of public discussion. Courage and honor are not subjects of literary controversy, but occasions of action."

Such was his passionate seriousness. And I do remember that, at the breakfast, he was still angry with Stewart for what he considered a misrepresentation of his own correspondence with Stewart, at last set in print in the book. I recall as well his repeating a conversation he once had with Eliot, a conversation which should (he said) have put him on guard against Stewart. Such was the point of his recollection of his conversation with Eliot, though not its content. I do not remember much of what Mr. Ransom had to say. I do recall that he and I, after the breakfast, stood chatting outside in the early Texas sunlight. We were watching a grackle almost at our feet. Its iridescent black feathers, its bright eyes, seemed some rescue of its awkward stumping about the grass looking for its breakfast, as if it were in leg casts or on stilts.

And I remember that during and after the breakfast, I was quite aware that these two poet-critics, famous among the anthologists and so in many classrooms here and abroad, were veterans of many old critical wars, waged before my time. I knew also that on occasion they had been more antagonists to each other than allies. Certainly on one occasion, Mr. Tate's anger had risen almost to the pitch of that explosion against the *Partisan Review* editor. That was the occasion of Mr. Ransom's review of Eliot's *Waste Land* in the *Literary Review* a few months after the poem's publication (the July 14, 1923, issue). Mr. Tate fired off an angry letter to Mr. Ransom, who responded as one sore offended. Tate wrote a fierce rebuttal to the *Literary Review*. Had I known at the time of the breakfast as much about that old issue between them as I believe I understand now, I should have been better tuned no doubt to nuances in our conversation. No doubt I would remember in more detail Mr. Ransom's rather quiet participation, and might have better appreciated Tate's recollection of his conversation with Eliot, which I now suspect was intended to carry the argument beyond Tate's discomfort with Stewart and his book.

They had made me a third with them, but I fear I was not sufficient to the inclusion. What follows, then, is my exploration of the old philosophical grounds of antagonism between them, which remained between them. I do not intend to set the one against the other as poets. I value the poetry of each as poetry, as I trust will be sufficiently evident in what follows. What concerns me is the disparate grounding of their faith in the virtues of well-ordered words. Their faiths are derived from quite separate philosophies about the word and its uses. I acknowledge in advance that my own faith is rooted in grounds close to those of Mr. Tate, remembering as well that he had a considerable struggle coming to those grounds. Through his struggle, my own intellectual journey has been in some degree made less arduous.

I might make a statement about those grounds in relation to the wars of words so conspicuous in our century. At the center of our intellectual wars is the disputed doctrine of the essential unity of intellect, in relation to the unified intellect of each person as included in the whole of creation and not separate from it. That is the orthodox position Tate comes to, but it is one which Ransom sets aside. The war between them on this point is one waged more widely than by our poets. It is central to the disarray of philosophy in this century. It permeated the emerging new science of psychiatry with which pre–World War II poets had to come to terms. It is present, though not usually recognized to be, in the social and political concerns of our day, affecting institutions and programs—whether the concern is with welfare programs or elections to public office. It is at the very heart of the destructive eruptions of wars in our century.

That is why the poets' engagements of the concern are of importance beyond the question of the aesthetic virtues of their poems as things in themselves. The virtue of poems as art depends on their nature as made things. For once made, a poem enjoys a certain independence of its maker, even as does man the maker from his own Creator. We are looking at two poets of considerable accomplishment, then, in respect to a question important to our century beyond the academic concern for the importance of poetry or literary criticism. And we shall be concerned as well with that other presence at our breakfast, then recently dead but whose presence must have been almost palpable to Mr. Tate and Mr. Ransom, given their old, fundamental disagreements about the word as it relates, in Mr. Eliot's suggestion, to the transcendent, "the word within the Word." And we shall look into such concerns from a position defined long ago by St. Thomas Aquinas, for whom the reality of the essential unity of intellect lay at the center of his own passionate concern. Were he with us (as in a sense he is) he would be alarmed at how thoroughly the Averroist heresy against the nature of intellect seems to have triumphed. He would no doubt find Siger de Brabant or his minions at every turn. It is in support of St. Thomas's position then that I take my own stand in the pages that follow.

I

The Setting Forth

First of all, my argument depends on my acceptance by faith of a principle that is decisive to the argument, a principle I believe formulates a central truth: man is in his primary nature an intellectual creature, whatever the range of intellectual gifts we may distinguish from person to person. This being true, it must follow that the intellectual actions of the discrete person, within the limits of that person's unique and discrete gift of intellect, will be cumulatively decisive to that person's well-being as intellectual creature. That is why we must always carefully value by intellectual reflection our inheritance from our intellectual fathers. It will mean concomitantly as well that the person's intellectual actions in a present moment effect in some manner the general well-being of the community of mankind in that moment. And that makes a double imperative to our address to the mixed gifts of our fathers. What we are addressing is the responsibility of the particular intellect to tradition. That responsibility is to preserve the viable out of the totality of its inheritance and strengthen it through those peculiar gifts whereby the individual is a person.

Depending as my argument does on faith in this principle, I ought to clarify my own understanding of the nature of faith which moves me to an acceptance of the principle. And especially I should do so, since it is my contention that all intellectual actions proceed out of faith. What then is *faith*? Here is a preliminary characterization, to which we shall return. Faith is an intellectual consent in some degree to the *possible*. As the possible emerges as more and more probable to the rational intellect (which is not of course infallible in its supposing the *possible* as *probable*), faith thereupon becomes strengthened in its focus of assent to the probable. That action of intellect is the necessary pursuit of the *actual*, of what *is*. Intellectual action, precipitated as it were by some degree of faith, is both supported by faith and supports faith, whatever perception of reality that faith holds.

But because finite intellect is fallible in consequence of its finitudes, it is possible that an intense and growing faith as justified by rational intellect may give inordinate consent to an illusion misunderstood as a reality. If this were not a possibility to the intellectual life, and indeed a probability in any active moment, the unfolding of the soul in its potentialities would be a determined process, an inevitability in a mechanist sense. In brief, then, I hold that even the intellectual action of radical nihilism is itself dependent on faith. It is out of faith that we now move to a concern for central questions always engaging intellect in its actions, and they are questions necessarily implicit in our concerns for nature or history or community. This is true, whether our position is that of Thomist, Idealist, Positivist, or whatever. To the mysteries of existence itself that stir faith in intellect, then.

There are two mysteries always confronting intellect in its attempts to understand its own existence, mysteries suggested by the two concepts *nature* and *history*. These are mysteries teasing to the intellect, whether it be committed to action under the rubrics of—and the accompanying sciences of—economics, politics, physics, biology, philosophy or theology. Nature in relation to *history* we discover to be the abiding and fundamental theme of intellectual action, and of course it is a very conspicuous theme in the writings of the Fugitive-Agrarians.

Let us begin by observing that the Medieval world had its own "big bang" theory about the relation of nature and history. It saw a fulfilling of caused creation, initiated by an explosive creative grace, whereby God said at the beginning "Let there be light." That vision

I. The Setting Forth

was subsequently appropriated, restricted, and refined in Renaissance thought and subsequent thought, but to intellectual ends whereby gradually human intellect itself emerges as the principal father of history. There is a considerable literature to which my metaphor speaks, and especially a literature that has recently concentrated on the Hegelian synthesis of this Renaissance inclination to establish intellectual autonomy in relation to nature. That development leads at last into a popular ideology—a popular negative theology—at the level of historical spectacle as established and popularized by Marx, and elaborated and executed by Lenin and their followers. But that we have come to "the end of history" as thus misrepresented, in the controversial metaphor of Francis Fukuyama, seems to leave us little the wiser for our long centuries spent wrestling with the causes of and consequences of our ideas.[1] That wrestling, in sum, has been with the question of history as the principle of order to the body of mankind, and we have come at the turn of the century to the alarming recognition of its inadequacy.

Given this summary context to our immediate concern, it seems to me one of the considerable ironies in contemporary "conservative" or "traditionalist" thought that this thought has recognized the errors leading to the modernist elevation of intellect as autonomous, whereby intellect would become the god of history, but too often attacks those errors from the limited ground of history itself as established by its opposition. That is to make the opposition to modernism vulnerable. If engaged from such a limited ground, the critique, given the recent urgency of necessity in such attempts (a fighting of fire with fire as it were), is often accompanied by a plaintive longing for rain in this dry season of our community's dissolution. Meanwhile the drought of "modernism" settles upon us. What I descry here are *ad hoc* defenses by traditionalists of intuited virtues of intellect, virtues which must be recovered to our health, and that is cause for rejoicing. But the longer there is reliance on the *ad hoc*, the more those defenses tend to become merely habitual and so ineffectual in the end. There is, after all, as we might say, a condition of knee-jerk "conservatism" no less than knee-jerk "liberalism" that occasions such *ad hoc* response. Such a response to the Platonic "negative theology" or modernism, then, must prove in the end insufficient, for it proves in the end an imitation of that negative theology.

The term "negative theology" seems both appropriate and useful to us in our effort to deepen our response to modernism. Eric Voegelin points out that Plato contributes the term *theology* to Western philosophical vocabulary. What is of interest to our present concern is that Plato, in the *Laws* and the *Republic*, is first of all concerned with negative propositions as types of theology. (Compare my remarks on faith in relation to nihilism.) There is an ignorance within the soul whose consequence is just such propositions, but the propositions in their effects influence public discourse and so public actions. That is why the fool who says in his heart there is no God must not be confused with the natural idiot. For when the fool as plausible intellect makes such declarations, careless intellects become intoxicated by the illusional freedom. They embrace such propositions as declarations of absolute independence.

We put the condition thus: the soul possesses illusions of truth accepted by faith as if visions of truth. As Eric Voegelin recognizes, whether intellectual action procedes from illusion or vision, those actions proceed out of faith.[2] It is for this reason that faith itself needs to be carefully considered at the outset, since the concern is with the conflicting engagements of differing faiths as the well-spring of intellectual action and conflict in community, whether held through negative theology (as does modernism) or positive theology (as does Thomistic realism).

Let us then make rather more clear what we mean by saying that faith is the ground of intellectual action. We shall define the term in what I understand as its proper aspect when governing intellectual deportment toward the abiding questions, here specifically the relation of history to nature. Faith is an openness of intellect, in some degree, to the unknown or to the only partially known: to that which includes but which is also inclusive of the faith-moved intellect. In

I. The Setting Forth

brief, faith is a deportment of intellect to existential reality—to the whole of creation signified as consequent to the "big bang," in whatever sense that initiating cause of being and of discrete beings is understood as effecting *what is*. Thus faith is the deportment necessary to any intellectual action, whether that positive deportment just described or a negative deportment out of negative theology in the Platonic sense.

Thus intellect is moved by faith, whether or not the unknown or partially known existential context to our intellectual response *is* in actuality. Whether in actuality it is an *other than*, but inclusive of the inclining intellect on the one hand. Or whether on the other hand it is an illusion spawned by our intellectual desire—a desire which by our given nature is intrinsic to intellect and gives rise to an inclination to some sort of rest in knowing the *other than*. In this respect, then, we say positively, if we are a Thomist, that faith is an initiating grace to which intellect consents because of its desire. Only thus is any intellectual action possible. We must add that faith is not determinate in its ends. For one may (and many do) rest faith in self-generated illusion, out of what is a false love of the self in the final reckoning. Faith is a response to grace's seeding of, the *in-fertiling* of, soul whereby the soul is granted its possible discovery of its teleological dimension. But it responds to the possible through its own intellectual actions which must be made proportionate to its own given, particular nature. Through this initiating grace, the journey toward beatitude is made possible to intellect, while a contingent possibility is a journey to that false beatitude, the elevation of the soul as autonomous and independent of even its own existential being through its willfulness, the alienated condition of self-love.

It is in the context of this thought that I see practical necessities to intellectual action if our intellectual community is to move toward its own viability in recovering the community of mankind. Thus the necessity of setting the problem of history in relation to nature, toward understanding the affairs of persons taken separately and in community. "There's a divinity that shapes our ends," Hamlet says in a distraught moment, "Rough-hew them how we will." In Shakespeare's day that "divinity" was understood to signify the God of creation, though with the growing effects of empiricism—that is, as the rough-hewing begins to appear more and more a fine tuning of nature (human and other)—that sense of "divinity" undergoes radical change.

In our day we largely understand the raw matter with which we ourselves shape our ends to lie immanently in material existence, requiring as the only acceptable divine power our finite intellect to process the possible ends we want effected. Thus process, emblematically celebrated as Progress (one of the Fugitive-Agrarian devil terms), becomes a symbolic naming of that new divinity, a shibboleth in the manipulation of the *hoi polloi* by gnostic intellect. And in this era especially, the new scholasticism of Progress in support of that divinity of autonomous intellect seems largely encompassed by that most recent among the sciences, economics. Such were the confused intellectual circumstances when the Fugitive-Agrarians began to respond. That is why it was inevitable that the Fugitive-Agrarians and the Distributists would attempt an alliance, their joint attempt represented by *Who Owns America?*, their less than satisfactory engagement of economic issues.

Modernist history then has its scholasticism. It is not concerned with the number of angels on a pinhead, as the popular deprecatory view of medieval scholasticism puts it. It is concerned rather with the variety of data speculatively abstracted from material existence in relation to the present stage of technology. Data is then speculatively related to history—to event—in the interest of a smooth-hewing of our material ends as our ultimate ends. The sacrifice made in the interest of this new scholasticism, practiced gnostically upon the material world, is the loss of a vision of the spiritual dimension of the speculator himself. By extension of effect it becomes the loss of that vision to the community of man which has more and more surrendered its intellectual consent to these new scholastics. One need consider only the elaborate industry in the American academy, rivaling the scholastic industry at the University of Paris in the 13th

I. The Setting Forth

century, to appreciate the concern. It has become an industry focused toward execution of scholastic programs through the power centered in political institutions along the Potomac as rationalized by academic scholastics.[3]

In this resolution through gnostic process which elevates Progress as the reigning divinity, there follows a loss of vision, and "Where there is no vision, the people perish." They perish as a people through embracing illusion out of a desire for vision, a condition suited to the machinations of gnostic intent to power over the ends to be shaped through intellect asserted as autonomous, as independent of causes other than itself. Against this destruction of the community of intellect, *ad hoc* resistance proves insufficient—again and again. Therefore, we must, as intellectual creatures, come to terms with both nature and history to recover our intellectual heritage from these manipulations of it. We can do so only insofar as we may effectively hold nature and history in a proper relation to each other. And that is possible only through metaphysics. Otherwise, we shall continue doomed to *ad hoc*, desperate attempts at recovery through inadequate appeals to either nature or history. More than history or more than nature as the ground of argument must be brought to bear upon our difficulties in this historical moment.

However, this is not to say that the complexities of history in its popular sense, which have fruited our scholarship, are to be sprayed by and sterilized by metaphysics, anymore than that we should approach nature with the false understanding of the uses of metaphysics as popularly understood. It is rather to say that we must depend less and less upon our continuing *ad hoc* "historical" response to historical modernism's abuse of community. We must enlarge the arena of our engagement with these enemies of a proper history and nature and science and philosophy and theology. These enemies to our intended recovery, let me suggest, have realized as if by an instinctive response to their own machination a terrible secret about mankind as temporally embattled in the ground of history and nature; in the limits of that ground, the present moment of history is always triumphant, so long as the engagement can be limited to a concept of history in which is denied any perspective upon it larger than its temporal dimensions.

If granted that limited ground as the limits of argument, the modernist is destined to triumph overlong, though not eternally, since by the authority of history so taken the present is self-evidently triumphant, though this moment's modernist is replaced by the next moment's. One might demonstrate that the triumph is not eternal, of course, by recourse to history, by the evidence again and again present in the sequences of moments past in which a presumption of triumph in that past moment now lie in decay. Not too long ago every school child was exposed to Shelley's ironic drama on this point in his sonnet "Ozymandias." It is a present view of past triumph. The two "vast and trunkless legs" of the monument stand in a desert, the anciently "modernist" inscription still legible: "My name is Ozymanidias, king of kings:/ Look on my works, ye Mighty, and despair!" The chilling hush of the desert settles on many a reader in the concluding words of the poet: "nothing beside remains. Round the decay/ Of that colossal wreck, boundless and bare/ The lone and level sands stretch far away."

Under the pressures of a "politically correct" curriculum, our young may soon be denied the chilling arrest of that moment. But they will not miss, eventually, its present manifestations. For they will encounter in most personal and specific ways that abiding metaphor—a fare of philosophy and literature that is ageless: the tensional fissures, in their present moment as an awakening generation, between themselves and their immediate fathers, whether actual fathers are present or not. And they will encounter in another perspective those eruptions between themselves and their own daughters and sons. Against that error ancient wisdom speaks: generations pass but the truth abideth.

It is truth as possible to intellect which puts history and nature in their proper perspective, their ordinate relationship to each other. The necessity is for a metaphysical vision to order community, lest

I. The Setting Forth

persons perish for lack of a vision of truth. That the necessity of metaphysical vision presses upon us more heavily than at any time since the 13th century seems self-evident. We may cite the concern of rigorous intellectuals as they resist the decay of intellectual community in our century. Thinkers as diverse as the particle physicist Niels Bohr and the philosopher Eric Voegelin recognize the necessity that we recover metaphysical vision.

What we mean by such a vision is a climate of consent among intellects, a presumption of truth as possible to intellect but not created by intellect itself. There is, by such a view, an intellectual insight of reality, the existential complex of reality which is always adjacent and always engaging intellect. But the view sees as well that intellect is a part of that complex and not its cause. Such vision allows intellect an anchor in some desirable but never perfect possibilities to its knowing reality. Never perfect, since intellect is itself a part of that whole which it must engage through its natural actions.

With such a consent on faith to the possibility of truth there may emerge a sufficiently common consent that makes intellectual discourse possible once more among the diversity of intellects now so much at odds. That discourse, by embracing a common good, will not therefore mean an absolute correspondence of vision between one intellect and another. But it does allow the possibility in the intellectual community, first of all, of a common recognition of truth as vouchsafed to intellect by reality itself. That will allow a communal consent beyond the presumption of isolated intellectual autonomy, beyond the presumption that intellect is the measure of truth rather than truth the measure of intellect. That gnostic dislocation has evolved since the Renaissance, we suggested, with the effect of atomizing the intellectual community into increasingly desperate and disparate assumptions of isolated self-sufficiencies. This effected subjectivism is self-willed as the limit of any intellectual certainty. Its destructiveness to the community of humanity is lamented in our epitaph for our age: the Age of Alienation.

II

Of Children and Kittens

Here at the turn of the 21st century, we have entered into intellectual civil wars in the name of concepts, posited and counter-posited concepts, without a sufficient anchoring of concepts in the realities of existence itself. That is my contention. None of those concepts are more volatile at the moment than *natural rights* and *natural law*, tearing apart the worn fabric of our political community. Though we may not hope to still the conflict, we may at least hope to mediate and lessen the destructiveness to some in the intellectual community itself. Perhaps we may at least clarify the neo–Thomist position, that of G. K. Chesterton, a father of Distributism, which he derived from the formal arguments of St. Thomas. Then we may relate that position to what the Southern Agrarians intuitively engaged in their concerns for nature and nature's history. For they recognized that both of these concepts were threatened by the dominant modernism of science and sociology, disciplines of mind that both Chesterton and the Agrarians tended to excoriate.

First, then, consider the Thomistic understanding as a background to our discovering something dependable about the Agrarians' intuited grounds of defense. Because it is intuited, we may not expect an orderly advance of argument comparable to the rational position of Thomism. Still we may, in juxtaposing two of those Agrarians, in the interest of an economy in our argument (John Crowe Ransom and Allen Tate), justify the intuitive, though it is not sufficient in itself. Indeed, it is St. Thomas who insists on the validity to thought of an initiating intuitive knowing. For him, rational

II. Of Children and Kittens

knowing is a subsequent *extension* of the intuitive. What we want to establish here is the appropriateness of and compatibility of that alliance of the continental neo-Thomists and Southern Agrarians which reached an uncertain focus in their joint collection of essays, Who Owns America? published in 1936. In that book the Chestertonian Distributists joined with the Agrarians in an attempt to correct the new science of economics in what they saw as its aberrant inclinations. They did so on behalf of nature itself. It is thus that their position set itself against both Marxism and a secular Capitalism, which were beginning to reach a climactic battle with each other in the 1930s. Such have been the ideological wars of our century, that among the confusions attendant on them has been a misunderstanding among some "capitalists" of the position taken by those Southern Agrarians toward industrialism as founded in capitalism.

We must come to a concern for natural rights, in relation to natural law, in attempting our clarification of their position. But we may do so effectively only by understanding first of all what the Thomistic realist means by his confident assertion that man is by his nature an intellectual creature first and foremost. For that is the position from which our argument advances. If man is such a creature, then his intellectual *nature* as a discretely existing creature within the whole of creation is our necessary point of departure toward understanding both nature and history. For it is man as intellectual creature whose principal burden is to understand. His intellectual action, the signal species of the action collectively termed "history," is consequential to man's own nature in its potentialities to the discrete person. But it is consequential also to nature as a whole. It is for that reason, then, that a preliminary reflection on intellect, in respect to epistemology as seen from the Thomistic perspective, precedes our turning to the embattled concepts of *natural right* and *natural law* as derived from human nature (man as intellectual creature) engaging the whole of nature by man's discrete intellectual actions.

It seems an observable aspect of our thinking as separate persons that, once we are intellectually engaged by a thing of nature, there follows a reflective response to the engagement. Such an initiating engagement we name *experience*, and reflection follows more or less upon experience. It is in this turning of intellect from experience itself to thought about experience that difficulty arises in maintaining our initial, the initiating, openness to the thing, an openness characteristic of human experience. For without some degree of openness, there is no experience available to intellect. Experience occasions the reflective turning from the present, from an actual encounter by intellect of *something*. In speaking of *openness*, I mean to emphasize it as always an active—not a passive—response of intellect to the discrete thing. This action of receptiveness to the discrete thing requires such a paradoxical naming. It is a *reaching toward* which is not thereby an aggression against nor a defenseless acceptance of the something to which intellect opens itself. Such is the movement out of faith. The balance needed in this encounter is an intellectual responsibility which is within the keep of the virtues of both the *thing itself* and of the active, reaching intellect. One experiences at a secondary level, by reflection, an absence of such balance, while recognizing as well the inclination to the action of receptiveness as always a present possibility. Consider, for instance, the rough loving by a child of a defenseless kitten. The sophisticated intellect standing by, the parent, is at once fearful for kitten and delighted by the child's actions, and that ambivalent response is a recognition of imbalance in the child's loving but possibly destructive openness to the kitten.

As any parent or any person in the position of mentor knows, such an ambivalent state of intellect bears in upon his responsibility. In our instance, our response to the child's delighted grasp of a defenseless kitten reveals an entanglement of our intellect in a present moment. In that moment we ourselves are at once held by the experience in a most personal way and pulled to a response beyond the event as personal only. We are prompted by intrusive reflections concomitant to the present event. Out of memory, more or less strengthened by the cumulative experiences of our encounters with things, we know the present arena thereby enlarged beyond what is

II. Of Children and Kittens

possible to the child. We know the complexity of the present event as the child cannot. This is to say that cumulative experience affects the limits of a present experience, with increasing complications to our reflective understanding of a present event. Indeed, this is the circumstance to intellect in its attempt to rescue "tradition" to present circumstances in order to make action in those present circumstances ordinate in relation to the truth of things.

By reflection, more or less ordered by our rational powers, we sort present experience in relation to memory of experiences, ours and our fathers', and in doing so at our best rescue the element of truth at the heart of remembered event. It is this problematic condition of intellectual action into which intrudes always the mystery of free will itself. Insofar as one is governed in his present intellectual response to a present event by the truth firmly held, he contributes to the viability of tradition. And here we must understand that we mean first of all the tradition characterized as the history of our own discrete experiences of nature. For such personal tradition is inescapable. In response to those experiences insofar as they are lighted by the testimony of other intellects, we maintain a suitable communal tradition. This is to say that the traditionalist is one who measures what is true in his own experience of nature by the cumulative knowledge of experiences, winnowed by rational reflection upon his own and his fathers' experiences. And that rational reflection obligates intellect to a measure of the knowledge held out of experience by his rational powers—corrected by intuitive knowledge. This in relation to an inherited testimony of knowledge held by his fathers and his fathers' fathers. Such is the condition of an acceptable community in time, which allows a balanced community beyond the immediacy of generations, beyond the present circumstance of one's child loving a kitten almost to death.

To return to that example after such a high prospect upon the history of generations is not the falling-off it might at first appear. For whether we admit it or not, the cumulative knowledge of experience bears upon any present experience, whether simple or complex. To come to such a realization, and to reorder intellectual action in our present moments, enables us to be more firmly reminded of our responsibility in the circumstance of the child loving the kitten. For the difference between the violence accompanying its antithesis, the desire for power over being, is a distinction necessary to any intellect in the responsible position of mentor. One recognizes, within the tradition as actively held, a difference between the accident of cruelty resulting from an act of love and cruelty to another of God's creatures wantonly committed. If one responds only to the plight of the kitten, he will make no such distinction, supposing only a wanton extremity: the wounding of the kitten. But if one regards the distinction within the traditional concern of intellect as steward of creatures (including children) rather than as master of creatures—that makes all the world of difference. The cliché here is quite intentional, since the health of all the world is an issue second only to the health of that little world, the person who is always at risk in his act.

The term *tradition* is much belabored in our own century, having become a shibboleth variously used, from the extreme use of it as a god term (which is my intent) to the use of it as a devil term—to recall Richard Weaver's apt distinction about such terms which he develops in *Ideas Have Consequences* and *The Ethics of Rhetoric*. The difficulty leading to the term's decay is not far to seek, in relation to what we are arguing about regarding the child and kitten, for how seductive the memory of our own encounters with kittens. (A reader may substitute any number of personal events in which the memory holds a transport of delight in response to some creaturely thing.) It is a temptation which, frozen, arrested in memory, effects that condition we call nostalgia. The "traditionalist" more or less frozen by nostalgia gives tradition a bad name in the midst of the *going-on-ness* of the present. Such failure to maintain tradition in the truth proper to the term, as properly received from our fathers and tested by personal experience, will thus contribute to the triumph of gnostic intent, the rejection of "history" save that of this present moment

II. Of Children and Kittens

governed by gnostic intent in the interest of the present autonomy of intellect.

Such a condition to the rescue of the true "thing" which we would call tradition makes maintenance of that true thing the bonding of community in time. Our failure of responsibility in this has perhaps never been more evident to the opening eye. In that recognition occurs the severe drawing of lines, between the radical antipathy of the visceral traditionist and the deliberate, rationalistic modernist. The symptoms of such an encounter are manifest at every hand, usually oriented at this moment in our concern for the collapse of the family, of our educational, judicial, legislative institutions, and so on. In the desperateness of the moment, under the conditions of what may be referred to as the meltdown of community, we better understand our inclination to *ad hoc* defenses of tradition. But if only *ad hoc*, they can seldom be effective. Our response is to a desire for that which is lost and becoming lost, when the response must properly be out of what is firmly established, so that it is neither lost nor need be lost: what is to be established is the fullness of the soul of the traditionalist himself. Within that (relative) fullness, we may recognize that in the world, fundamental causes are neither won nor lost by the power of intellect alone. For intellect is not the cause of the continuous going-on-ness of this present complex, existential reality.

It is this reflection, turned to meditation, that reveals to us that such are the conditions always present with intellect. Such are the conditions to be accepted by the (relatively) mature intellect in response to other intellects, also only relatively mature. The delicate balance in the exercise of any concern for the less mature than oneself, in respect to the gifts of intellect, is the most difficult balance to maintain, as any parent or teacher knows. It is such an understanding, however, sustained by viable tradition, that gives a proper perspective upon the child with the kitten, to speak figuratively. In that understanding one sustains the love in any encounter, without distorting excess. One does not on the instant strike the child who is unwittingly choking the kitten nor snatch the grasped kitten from the child, thus breaking the kitten's neck. One mediates as steward of event. One imitates, always imperfectly, the Omniscience of which we are images. That is the discomforting responsibility of each person.

III

Getting at the Truth: The Nature of Intellect in Act

In the reflective response to an intellectual experience of a particular thing, such are the limits to rational intellect (in distinction from the intuitive intellect which is initially dominant in a child's response to things) when the thing in itself seems arrested by reflection upon the fading experience of encounter with a thing. It is important to note this distinction between the rationally reflective action of intellect and the open immediacy of intuitive intellect which we call an experience of a thing. It is a distinction that allows us to understand the seeming arrest. For this seeming arrest of the thing itself is deceptive to rational intellect in respect to the reality of the thing. We seem to experience an arrest, but this is consequent to the intentional attempt of rational intellect to comprehend the thing, in the literal sense of *comprehend*, to seize and hold the fullness of the thing. This seeming experience of arrest so affected the recent philosopher of language Brice Parain that in his *Metaphysics of Language* he declares it the effect of the act of naming the thing. "When we name something," he says, "we in fact kill it." However, neither the naming nor the reflection "kills" any thing in itself through the act of intellectual engagement of the thing.

Let us make yet another distinction. The arrest as effected by reflection seems also an arrest of intellect itself, with the accompanying sense to intellect of its isolation, its being set aside from all things other than itself. But we may distinguish this condition of intellect in its existence, its sense of an isolation consequent upon experience itself when thought engages the experience, from a lingering and disturbing remembrance of the condition of intellect as it *was* within the experience itself. It *is not*, on reflection, how it was. Intellect knows a difference in its prior condition of being, attendant upon and consequent to experience, and its succeeding condition of being once it reflects upon its knowledge of having had an actual experience of some thing. Nevertheless, in reflection, it yet bears a lingering, a continuing intuitive knowing, about the past experience in its past actuality which its present reflective, its "rational" engagement of experience, cannot fully recover. What is lingeringly known to intellect is the actuality of a visionary relation of itself to a thing within limiting circumstances. That visionary sense, a memory of openness in an event, differs from a now present attempt to recover that desirable condition.

The remembered condition seems similar to the present arrest seemingly caused by reflection, but a crucial difference is the faint recollection that within the moment of the experience itself, now past, intellect seemed then untouched by arrest, or at least by arrest of the same nature as this present arrest through reflective isolation. The culprit occasioning that difference is likely to be named *thought*, or at least it is likely to be so named within the tradition of philosophy we speak of as "romanticism." Not the philosopher, but the poet engages this disparity between the two arrests of intellect in an immediately accessible way, and so we shall turn to the poet here. That poet is likely to characterize the lost state of intellect as an ideal stasis, a balance in *being* through intellectual encounter of things. He dramatizes that loss, and in doing so he is most easily tempted toward nostalgia, so that attempts, as reflected in his dramas, very likely bear the emotional character of pathos. Such is the "romantic" aspect of much of our poetry since the 18th century. But we are ill-advised to reject what is intrinsic to that art with the pejorative epithet, mere "romanticism."

III. Getting at the Truth: The Nature of Intellect in Act

For some purchase on our point, recall the celebrated "romantic" poet William Wordsworth. A considerable theme in his life's work is the disparity between reflective arrest and the seemingly "active" event, the experience as remembered within an arrest. The condition of his soul which he would celebrate he called "spots of time." Our own era's "romantic" poet, T. S. Eliot, engaging the same difficulty, came to speak of "still points." Their sense of the lost spot or point, in which they somehow escaped time, is that it is the most desirable state of all to intellect, a state of harmony of intellect and thing within a context accepted, a balanced resolution of particular existences (intellect and thing) within being itself. Our mystics late and soon attempt to characterize such "moments" which are of indefinite duration in relation to time as a surface to such existence. Those moments are temporal rescue of soul toward a final timeless, enduring "moment" beyond both time and space. And that condition is variously named by both poets and mystics, though in the West it is usually named the beatitude of the soul, experienced analogously through spots or still points of time.

As for the more easily understood experience of arrest consequent to reflection upon experience, an arrest out of such spots or points, that reflection tells us that it is indeed an effect *in* and *to* intellect, and as intellectual creatures we attempt to riddle the condition responsibly. We recall here a celebrated attempt by the poet to understand the difference between his experience of a timeless moment and his decay into time's arrest of intellect by his reflection: John Keats's "Ode to a Nightingale." The poem opens with the divisive effect upon the heart of the action of the head, *thought* characterized as the source of sorrow and "leaden-eyed despair." We need not explore the poem at length, but it is clear that, dramatically, the words of the poem follow a seemingly timeless moment of balance between intellect and a thing, the nightingale, from which words themselves wake the speaker.

The words seem intuitively spoken at first, a cry of regret. But the rational dimension of that cry becomes more and more dominant, rational thought contending with the imagination's attempt at intuitive words. The fading experience is but "One minute past," and the poem unfolds as an attempt, through the imaginative command of thought, to recover that moment. Imagination proves inadequate to the attempt, so that at the end, in the concluding words on the brink of despair, the speaker is uncertain whether the minute past, the still point of rapture to intellect within its experience of a thing (the nightingale and its song), was within the country of true reality or whether this present condition of despair in time and place is the only reality. What seemed actual in the still point seems most probably to the poet but wishful thinking. ("Was it a vision or a waking dream?") Despair out of the division of intellect from thing through thought is the inescapable burden, which cannot be shifted from that intellect by "beauty" imaginatively conjured, though such is the poet's attempt. (I have explored this intellectual dilemma at length in *Romantic Confusions of the Good: Beauty as Truth, Truth Beauty*.)

In attempting to riddle this arrest by our rational pursuit of lost moments, encouraged by our recollections of still points of experience intuitively known in this moment and now lingeringly remembered, we shall better understand the danger involved when rational intellect elevates itself as the god of being through its "science," its knowing of things as if comprehensive of things, to the exclusion of intuitive knowing. What occurs is perhaps rather a violation in some degree of the reality of the thing itself as well as of the operative intellect. Or at least a violation may follow in consequence of actions in nature that follow from the misunderstanding. Indeed, this is the arena of the physical manipulation of things by gnostic intent, against which the Agrarians set themselves.

Indeed, this is the fundamental concern underlying their suspicions of the new science whose triumph was certified by an industrialism that was rapidly transforming community into desperate consumers of things. The reality of the experience is, in truth, rather a loss of the proper relation of intellect to that thing. The change in actuality is first of all a change from the openness of intellect itself

III. Getting at the Truth: The Nature of Intellect in Act

to the thing, a change consequent upon its reflective recognition of that event of encounter through that initial openness which is the experience of the thing itself by intellect. Now intellect, among the things it knows, knows this as a difficulty. It knows that this is the crux of its relation to things other than itself. Indeed, it may well be that this particular knowing is the cause of our intellectual dependence upon analogy as an attempt to overcome the effect of arrest through signs. By our word, we may overcome a seeming isolation of intellect. That address of sign to the recovery from isolation engages the mystery of memory of encounter.

We may see the point perhaps in relation to the greatest challenge of all to intellect, its enlarging its response to the complex of existential reality which is beyond the limited knowing of particular creatures—particular things. For intellect is engaged by a desire to know the totality of creatures, the whole of creation. Thus it is that the growing discoveries of particle physics in the 20th century, focused upon the mystery of the *thingness* of elementary matter, seems suitable to an attempt by analogy to know the wholeness of creation itself. It is an instance of this abiding inclination of intellect to analogy, prompted by the sense we have of the thoroughness of theoretical particle physics. We at least *comprehend* minute existence, or so we are inclined to suppose. To know the atom thus seems a way of knowing the whole bang of being by the correspondences in analogy. By the attempt of analogical mediation, then, out of our (mistaken) sense that we possess a comprehensive knowing of the thingness of the particle, we incline to think it suitable vehicle to our enlarged attempt to grasp the thingness of all creation, a sense of all creation as an entity. Also, by analogy, we might thereby mediate thought's seeming arrest of that *going-on-ness* of creation in its totality which we intuitively recognize but which yields inadequately to our limited reflective approach to the whole of creation. It is in this light, for instance, that we glimpse the intent of Wordsworth's suggestion that the poet precedes and follows after the man of science. It may also, perhaps, suggest why among particle physicists at the turn of our century there has been increasingly a concern for recovering a metaphysical vision appropriate to the intricacies of their growing physical vision of particle reality. For they, being the most knowledgeable in the specialization of knowing, recognize their "science" as inadequate to the mystery they engage.

"In truth," we say, "I know this or that." Such is our way of saying that the mode of the essence of *this* or *that* is truth held in intellect. We hold such truth, even though we do not put it in such scholastic terms. For we realize that the essence of the thing is not itself *in* intellect. If it were, we should then be the god of the thing; we should then, by the power of our own intellect, be the Lord and Giver of life to the thing so held. To make that point is to be reminded of "scientists" who sometimes suppose their own minds to be the receptacle of essences of things and from that supposition move to radically affect reality by an alteration of essence itself. It is at the moment, for instance, a dangerous tendency in the otherwise welcomed science of genetics. The inclination to a confusion in our thought between the truth of a thing and the essence of a thing persists, a confusion occasioned by inadequate thought or by a presumption by will to usurp godhead in becoming the Prime Cause of things. For we are by the freedom in our nature as intellectuals capable of either a careless or a willful gnostic address of intellect to things.

In the larger context of creation, there is a participation in cause and effect which is tensionally operative in creation. The intricate and so often mysterious relation of essences as the ground of the active being of things constitutes relationships not mediated by thought to the disparate things, a truth difficult to accept because of gnostic intent. Each existing thing is an already *given*, namely its peculiar nature. The non-intellectual things of creation in respect to truth as held by intellect is not of a concern to the non-intellectual thing in its own relation to its context; at least it is not in the same manner as it is a concern to the intellectual creature. But nevertheless, this relationship of a tensional support of creation as a whole within

III. Getting at the Truth: The Nature of Intellect in Act

itself, when seen by intellect in our enlarged perspective, involves the participation by intellectual creatures with the nonintellectual creatures in the ground of being itself. This is to speak then of the contextual *going-on-ness* of creation as existing under the purview of divine law, as St. Thomas would put it. The inclusive—the comprehensive—relationships among the totality of things, in this perspective, is that of the *fatherhood* of God to the *childrenhood* (the *creaturehood*, the *created natures*) of the multiplicity of things. The particular natures of discrete things, then, constitutes the whole of creation in a tensional complex. It is this context in which the intellectual creature man moves and has his primary intellectual being, and he does so by virtue of his peculiar nature, he having been made in the image of God. But his finitude as "image" and his freedom of will complicate his becoming through the response of his will to truth as held through grace by intellect.

Thus we continue to be confronted by a seeming impasse to intellectual comprehension of the wholeness of any entity, made rather spectacularly obvious in our attempt to comprehend the universe as an entity. Nevertheless, the intellect's desire to do so by its action is always present in our attempt to know either the whole or some distinct entity out of that wholeness, any discrete specific thing itself. By an enlargement of the problem with this local—this discrete adjacent thing encountered by *experience*—to the level of a universal intent to a comprehension of being, we may discover the limit to the focus of thought itself upon any existential thing, from the particle to the whole of creation. We recognize a necessary totality to any singular thing which is nevertheless itself at once limited and bracketed by and included in the totality of existing things. Thus we may know intuitively, and perhaps even accept at last as an actuality to intellectual action itself, the limited power of intellect to comprehend. This is one way we move toward accepting the intuitively known existence of a Power of Comprehension, God, who alone is capable of the comprehension we as images of that omniscient power desire. To do so is to be moved by the virtue of our nature as beings created in the image of that Comprehending Power. We may be moved to an acceptance of our own finitude as creatures, however gloriously taken that finitude may be. And we may do so joyfully, escaping the threat of despair occasioned by pride.

We turn from reflection on the whole—the totality of creation or the totality of any singular creature included in that totality. By that action, reflective thought itself seems arrested from the going-on-ness of the being of a thing and of the whole of things. Thus we may find ourselves recovering an awareness once more of that largeness beyond comprehension, the going-on-ness of the whole of creation. Thus we may again turn in an openness to some particular, immediate, adjacent, local thing.

Such is the continuing rhythm to intellectual action. In the small compass of our relation by the intellectual action of openness to the atom, for instance, or to a discrete organic creature like a kitten or a stone or the like, we respond knowingly to the dynamics of that particularly discrete entity thus engaged. This is the intellectual openness St. Thomas meant in reminding us of our own experiences: human intellect is capable of attending actively only to the singular finite thing as engaged with immediacy by intellect. It is only the singular thing that profits intellectual understanding through cumulative experiences, but it does so far short of intellect's *comprehending* any thing. The conglomerating, reflective action of intellect upon its disparate encounters, however, tempts a supposition of comprehension.

It is through the singular, St. Thomas says, which is initially mediated by the senses, that we may and must (while limited by our temporal and spacial finitudes as intellect) approach the Cause of all finitude. Out of local singular encounter we move to a recognition of God. The endangerment implicit in that necessary approach occurs through our limited intellectual faculty as commanded by will, as when we attempt to comprehend the totality of a discrete creature or the totality of creation in a presumption of the autonomy of intellect. And so it is in this attempt at comprehension, as opposed to

III. Getting at the Truth: The Nature of Intellect in Act

accepting a limited knowing, that we are given to making a dynamic whole appear to intellect as a static entity. But the arrested oneness is a supposition in the intellect itself and not in the thing which occasions the response of our reflective arrest.

It is in this dilemma, I believe, that we nevertheless find ourselves again and again restored from what is by its effect an arrest of intellect itself and not an arrest of the thing in itself. And we are restored by the grace of the Comforter, the Holy Ghost. That Lord and Giver of life is always and at once present as Cause in the going-on-ness of the discrete entity. We are enabled by grace to approach things by our intellectual action, including the essential going-on-ness of our own discrete existence as intellectual creature. Thus is restored momently the relation of intellect to thing, whereby the truth of the thing is held by intellect, that truth being a mode of the existential reality which is appropriate to finite intellect. By analogy there is a correspondence between the essence of the thing in itself and truth as the mode whereby essence is perceived in the surrogate of essence, truth, held by intellect. There is, then, this continuingly available action of the grace of mediation to our intellect in its experience of the thing. That is the gift of the Lord and Giver of life. It is a mediation of the going-on-ness, continuous in the whole of creation. Thereby we may say that things exist and so things always await an acceptance through intellectual openness, an openness mediated by experience through faith. It is continually, though not continuously, available to intellect through right will. Because it is not continuous, the intellect, sensitive to its possession of the truth of things out of experience, delights in spots of time and lives in hope of a continuous experience of openness, Beatitude.

It is as intellectual creatures gone astray through mistaking our own distortion of reality, effected by a desire to possess reality by knowledge, that we mistake the limits of finite understanding as if it were comprehensive of beings. We nevertheless are always enabled to begin over, always by grace allowed a restoration of the potential of our finite intellect of an immediate experience through openness. If we put the point in relation to deliberate willfulness, to that gnostic intent to power over being that each intellect is susceptible to, we may say that such is the grace operative in us through our confession, contrition, and amendment of the will that we may be restored again and again beyond our repeated gnostic falling away from actual being.

It is reassuring to realize as well that we act out this re-beginning of intentional spiritual reformation by a re-beginning of intellectual action in response to created things. Thus we turn by openness to the discrete creature, always here and now, in an acceptance of its existence as discrete creature. Such is the endearing advantage we tend to witness and envy in the small child, as that child embraces a puppy or kitten. But we are aware as well, through cumulative experience, that the same child may with the same openness embrace the poison berry. The juxtaposition of puppy and poison berry reminds us that as created intellectual creatures with free will, distinguishing us from berry or puppy, we are required by our given nature to make intellectual distinctions among things. We are, rationally, responsible to our experiences. Through such labor we recognize and value properly the discreteness of the created thing, whether of ourselves or puppies or berries.

And here we have characterized the intellectual piety required of a right will, lest the will violate the particular virtues of any discrete thing including itself: lest we transgress upon the going-on-ness within the complex of the discrete thing as it both exists in itself and within the going-on-ness of all creation. Only thus is it possible at last to honor with appropriate intellectual conduct the existential reality of discrete and separate things, whether puppy or poison berry or child. This movement then from openness to each thing in itself to reflection upon the consequentially known but incompletely comprehended truth of the thing: this is the tensional ground to our discrete intellectual action as a person so long as intellect is alive. It is the tensional spring to intellect, making possible its journey to its potential perfection, which in its superlative designation we call Beatitude.

IV

The Mystery of Nature and the Brooding Breast of Love

In the play of human thought between the intuitive immediacy of intellect to things and the reflective response to that experience, desire may lead intellect astray. We know an inevitable concept that our intellect at some times and under some conditions attempts to establish as an actual past or potential future reality. It is a concept, given a figurative name, which we entertain in response to the difficulty we have in riddling the mystery of "Mother Nature," to put another popular figurative term as the name for that complex totality containing the mystery. I mean the concept of *Eden*. It is that concept that tempts intellectual nostalgia on the one hand, a remembering backward through the hazes of events in nature as remembered in intellect. Or it is the concept, disguised by the presumption of intellectual autonomy, which makes us suppose that we may, by force of our will exercised on nature at its surface, create Eden in some future point. The proliferation of Utopian dreams, based in the moment's science, is a significant residue of our intellectual history, especially in the post–Renaissance world. We hardly need to be told with what anguished antipathy the resolute intellect which is nostalgic for Lost Eden and the equally resolute intellect bent on creating New Eden next year confront each other, usually counter-labeled as "romantic" and "realist." We may need to be reminded, however, how often both these intellectual stances toward the mystery of nature prove resident within our own, singular intellect.

On either hand, whether one be devoted to nostalgia or to utopian creationism by intellect, if we consider those inclinations from a Christian perspective on the mystery of nature, we detect in them nevertheless a suitable desire which has been distorted by intellect itself in its pursuit of a rest in truth. Whatever the supposed end to which these Edenic intellects are drawn, whether they are drawn out of this always-abiding presence of their being to a past or to a future, what the Christian suggests is that they are moved by a desire for union with the Cause of all being. The intellectual inclination is to orient the soul in its longing by a past moment now lost through its grievous error in the old garden, or by a future moment to be effected by intellect itself as a dreamed garden. In either distortion of desire, intellect becomes mired in time and space, prevented those moments of grace we called "spots of time." Thus the soul becomes mired in the surfaces of the mystery of nature as a whole.

Such are the immediate conditions of a quicksand to the soul, temporal and spacial obstacles it finds difficult to cross in its journey. For the soul through its helpmeet intellect cannot go *around* the continuous surface of being as a particularized creation, a surface which is coextensive to intellect in its relation to the whole of nature. The intellect as helpmeet may attempt to do so by radical illusion, the illusion of a nostalgia glazing that present surface as with a supposed ancient light now lost and lamented. Or it may by direct assault attempt to reconstitute that quicksand by its gnostic power, the imposed cement of will. Such attempted circumventions of the always intrusive reality of existence, in this always present moment of the soul, will in the end make more emphatic the inescapable circumstances to our discrete, particular, finite existence as person. That existence is in relation to finite existences constituting a quicksand to intellect when its knowing rests only on the surface of reality.

Let us for a moment consider, by speculative reflections, this quicksand, and in relation to the finitudes, both *of* and *in* existential reality—the conditions to our present moment of an active intellectual engagement of the mystery of nature. We begin from a Thomistic

IV. The Mystery of Nature and the Brooding Breast of Love

position and will return to the position, whether the present attempt to come to terms with this quicksand prove orthodox or not in every particular. The attempt is at least a dramatization of the sort of risk intellect must always take in its attempt to come to terms with the abiding mystery of nature, a nature which in dire moments will indeed seem not only nominally but actually a quicksand.

It is in response to such a perception of "nature" at the surface, the physical dimension of nature as opposed to the metaphysical dimension, that the various sciences rise through our intellectual labors. Those attempts are from different quarters of intellect's possible approaches to those mysteries. The approach is made by each intellect according to rational gifts.

The excesses of "science" rise under the illusions of intellectual autonomy consequent to those intellectual attempts to drain the swamp of nature in order to pass over dry shod, and we are always at risk by our temptation to such excess. But it is also in response to this perception and to our attempts through the disciplines of science that an intellect may properly order its own science in accord to its peculiar gifts. One recognizes the presence of grace to such attempts, and never more so than when presumption is rebuffed by reality. We proceed, then, with caution, insofar as prudence may support that caution and so support our speculative concern to move beyond the limits of our necessary sciences.[4]

Let us begin with a Thomistic concept, derived from our immediate experience of the swamp of objective reality by that formidable intellect, St. Thomas Aquinas. The concept is *natural rights*. The term speaks to that complex of the relationship of existential things, but it does so, St. Thomas advises, under the authority of divine law, not of a human management of law. What a difficult and ambiguous suggestion, this. For to human intellect there is not revealed in nature itself—in the totality of creation nor within discrete parts of that totality—an equilibrium among "rights" as supposed relevant to the actual natures of discrete things. Without that balance, how may we conclude that "divine law" is just? In the absence of such equilibrium,

45

little wonder that the divine law in its actualities seems to call into question both God's justice and His mercy. It is in response to these seemingly unequal laws of nature in relation to discretely existing things in their tensional involvement with each other that first God's justice, then His mercy, and eventually His very existence, is called into question by finite intellect. There seldom appears to human perceptions of events, as experienced, an equality of justice or mercy in nature consonant with finite intellect's sentimental—that is, self-centered—suppositions about the "rights" deemed appropriate to the discrete entities of creation.

If in moments we dream of Eden past or passing or to come, we may do so as if Eden were some island in a remote sea, whereon the constituting things of that island are in equilibrium. We do so in response to our present recognition of the confusing realities circumscribing our own present finite point, our stand within the whole of creation. From that point, within the center of the self, our perception that there is an absence of balance leads us to characterize an inequality as the principle of "nature." (Tennyson, with something of a shock to some Victorian sensibilities, speaks of nature as "red in tooth and claw.") It is in relation to this inescapable and testing point, to which we are returned again and again despite any dreams of past or future, that we *know* tensional effects of events. Most immediately the event we know is our own intellectual engagement at this present moment as circumscribed not only by present time and local place, but contained in some sense, at least by implication, by the large whole of creation. We "feel" thereby the pressure of a closed system of which we are the uneasy center. It is this tensional condition of our being which turns us to concomitant events of and to other things in creation, including those occasioned by our own presence. Such is the constitution of the complex "history" of this moment, the tensional complexity of events in this always present totality of creation that may seem to rest upon us.

This is the moment in which we experience the active overflow of and responsive encounters with essences of things, each to other.

IV. The Mystery of Nature and the Brooding Breast of Love

And so we attempt to speak analogically toward the larger complex of the tensional history of being in this moment, the totality of creation. We contemplate a whole by such analogy as that of Dame Julian of Norwich, who sees this whole in the small hazelnut on her palm: "I looked ... and thought, 'What may this be?' And it was generally answered thus: 'It is all that is made.' I marvelled how it might last [i.e., exist in this continuing present moment], for methought it might suddenly have fallen to naught for little[ness]. And I was answered in my understanding: 'It lasteth, and ever shall for that God loveth it.' And so all thing hath the Being by the love of God."

Little wonder, then, our temptation to Edenic desires, if we lack Dame Julian's visionary understanding. For one of the things intellect almost inescapably supposes from its always present encounter with reality is the absence of a perfected equilibrium distributed in being by the love of God. However it may be, thus the reassuring rest of a moment, a spot of time, through the mysterious existence of a hazelnut which does not in this moment fall "to naught for littleness." That is not to say that intellect may not attempt to establish its own equilibrium, its own accommodation to this overflow of tensional encounters in the present moment. It makes attempt through the actions of its own nature as intellect. That leads intellect, for instance, from reflection to meditation, to contemplation and thereby perhaps to the peaceful ordering of the soul as it is accommodated to whatever immediate thing it holds, not simply in the palm, but in an openness of intellect. Or so the Christian mystics instruct us. What we are more apt to know, short of such a still point of peace in contemplation, is that seemingly uneven flow of events, now favoring one creature over another, one people over another, one person over another.

The spectacle of such overflow—the fire, famine and flood of tensional encounters, to speak figuratively—reveals temporal ascendancies and recessions of things in relation to each other, which we are sometimes pleased to call the flux of nature. Consider as an instance our agitated environmental concerns at the turn of the 21st century, the popular address to the mystery of nature in this present confluence of events. The intent of the concern is too largely an unreasonable demand—by rebellious intellectual reactions against God as unjust—for an equilibrium, for a justice in creation. The intent of the justice we would impose in creation is out of a presumption that justness can be established by intellectual fiat and thereby effect all creation as Eden. One notes with a sense of irony that the specialists devoted to that concern for "natural" justice depend upon the scholasticism of computer models, illustrated in miniature by those popular small shrines, the living room aquarium or terrarium.

It is most difficult for intellect to come to terms with the continuous flow of contingent events, for alas there comes the morning after a night's power failure. There is the aquarium unaerated overnight: the complex of creatures floating on the dead surface of the lean water. Or the terrarium is neglected and the contending orders become unbalanced in a war. Despite such lessons out of the mystery of nature, however, it is still difficult to come to terms with the mystery of the tensional complex of creation as beyond any possible human law. It is difficult to accept the context as multitudinously active with event, out of the essential natures of the contingent things constituting the whole of creation. That whole is properly the purview of a divine law whose dimension of justness is beyond human comprehension. But not beyond understanding. And it is never more difficult to resolve disquiet with our failures of comprehension than in such moments of "history" as our own at the beginning of the 21st century, in which the dominant religion is a secularism bent on gnostic dominance over being as the only justice. Out of that intent there have emerged more sophisticated festivals with suitable shrines to Autonomous Intellect than Robespierre ever dreamed possible.

The struggle as we presently witness it reveals the attempt to derive out of secular gnosticism a paganism which must appear when put in perspective against the larger mystery of creation as at once comic and pathetic. We attempt to establish a religion accommodating intellect with creation by that secular thought whose operative prin-

IV. The Mystery of Nature and the Brooding Breast of Love

ciple is intellectual autonomy, based in partial encounter with the awesome flow of being. We are trapped within the surface flow of "nature," and so we lose the revelation of Dame Julian's chestnut: that being is the deepest mystery of all. Here and there, perhaps, one finds a lone soul recovering an orientation to the mystery of being somewhat. We may meditate on the calming words of Gerard Manley Hopkins, for instance. The world, he reminds us, is "charged with the grandeur of God"—by divine law. And so

> It will flame out, like shining from shook foil;
> It gathers to a greatness, like the ooze of oil
> Crushed.

That *gathering* succeeds always the *crushing*, at which we have become so adept at accomplishing through our present technologies. But for Hopkins, and of necessity for the orthodox Christian, "nature is never spent," though

> Seared with trade; bleared, smeared with toil;
> And wears man's smudge and shares man's smell ....

In this view, through meditation and contemplation, one sees that.

> There lives the dearest freshness deep down things ....
> Because the Holy Ghost over the bent
> World broods with warm breast and with ah!
> bright wings.

It is from such a moment of respite that we now may turn more formally to the question of *natural rights* as orienting the orders of beings called *nature* and to the concerns of that peculiar order of nature's beings, mankind, whose always salient concern is for a communal order sufficient to mankind's principal temporal responsibility, his office as steward of things (including himself) within the sustaining grounds of being.

Of Natural Rights and Natural Law: A Speculative Beginning

We tend, relatively late in Western thought, to the personification of the whole of creation, and the epithet most common is "Mother Nature." It is an ambiguous epithet, conducive to careless thought in that it trades upon our hunger to worship, a proper hunger in the soul. But when not governed by some understanding of the "nature" of existential reality, that inclination leads us to idol worship. We discover this inclination increasingly pervasive of the popular mind in this era. It is revealed, for instance, in a pseudo-sophisticated paganism which centers upon crystals or pyramids. The popular press regularly shows us gatherings of people at a geographical point at some remove from the world of man. Confused intellects gather to conjure a concentration of the "spirit" of nature.

There is another, scientifically girded paganism also—presently most appealing to a wandering and distraught intelligentsia—which issues in "Mother Nature" transformed to the goddess *Gaia*. Through the desire for an *essential* unity of all creation (that modern version of the Averroistic heresy of the essential unity of intellect), all creation is declared holy, a self-contained One. It is supposed holy of and in itself. It is as if by a willed desire, our inherited supposition of the universe as mechanistic (bequeathed us by 19th century scientism), we might thus inspirit creation with a vague humanism. Insofar as one is able to consent to such an attempt upon the reality of

V. Of Natural Rights and Natural Law: A Speculative Beginning

existential creation, human intellect may prove acceptable as the Holy Ghost sustaining reality. Such is the attempt dramatized by the spectacle of the French Revolution orchestrated by Robespierre, as in his establishing a "Festival of the Supreme Being" to apostatize rational intellect. That divination of intellect has in our century been supported by appropriations from the sciences, those sciences accepted as the scholasticism needed to establish a modern version of an ancient paganism, for worship by the popular mind.

Thus geology, chemistry, physics, biology, and so on are brought to bear upon the modern attempt to inspirit matter by the power of finite intellect. Thus we would lift ourselves by our own bootstraps, for thus it seems acceptably visionary through gnostic intent to declare autonomous intellect the Holy Ghost descended upon the universe from which it rose, justifying that strange necessity, borne within intellect itself beyond all attempts to exorcize it, to worship *something* beyond the discrete self. Out of a doctrine of spiritual immanence in matter, a reaction to the despair attending the 19th century vision of matter as mechanistically ordered and without transcendent cause, we suppose a recovery of a moral dimension to matter in the extensions of that principle. One need only explore the enthusiasm of some poets on encountering Henri Bergson's theory of "creative evolution," the mystery of an *élan vital*, to realize how welcomed is the prospect of a recovery of moral order to the universe after the studied rejection of the transcendent. Such was Bergson's effect, for instance, on poets as diverse as Robert Frost, Ezra Pound, and the young T. S. Eliot. For the severing of immanent and transcendent had been a cumulative effect upon Western thought out of a rationalism whose intent was, initially, to separate the "self" from creation in the interest of power over creation. The consequent alienation of intellect from things reached a spiritual crisis among intellectuals at the turn of our century. At this century's beginning the separation has extended a sense of spiritual crisis down to the popular mind.

Put another way, we approach a culmination of the progress of

18th century rationalism, through the Darwinian mechanistic reductionism of being, until with some desperation we require a new creationism, a transformation of the world by desire as gnostically controlled. The world as god is currently celebrated through a romanticizing of science. Consider to the point the celebration of the world as god revealed in James Lovelock's popular *The Ages of Gaia: A Biography of the Living Earth*. The title shows this work a species of a new hagiography, of which there are many, and many yet to come.

Now we must begin with a recognition that, as already suggested, the inclination that leads us to the confusion of science as the only metaphysics, employed in supporting the new paganism, is an inclination proper to the nature of man as intellectual creature. The inclination is not wrong. The problem is the failure to support that inclination by a right will in the exercise of reason toward intellectual clarifications of the inclination. And that confusion is what we shall attempt to address in relation to the currently obsessive concerns for natural rights and natural law in the political and social arena. It is in this arena of the larger complexity that we meet with an increasing sense of crisis to the sanity of community concerns.

My opening epigraph intends to speak toward our propensity to consent to intellectual limit in relation to "Mother Nature," recognized by the child, though the intellectual climate of our moment works diligently to exorcise that intuitive knowing in the child suggested by my analogy to a very old children's game. In that game, there is a progress of children from a starting line to the feet of the elected "director" of the game, the current "It" of the game, who exercises absolute power within the confines of the game itself. It is a progress determined by the grace of the "It" to the individual child. "Joseph (or Mary), take one giant step (or baby step or frog hop)." The centering of the relation of Joseph to the "It" lies not only in the grace of consent of the "It" but in the manner of acceptance of that gift by Joseph. His is a request to do what has been already allowed by the "It": "Mother, may I?" What makes the game exciting to all the players is the danger of impatience in the progress. For whichever

V. Of Natural Rights and Natural Law: A Speculative Beginning

child first reaches the Lord of the game becomes the Lord of the next game, becomes the "It." The excitement of the progress often makes a Joseph act out the gift of movement before asking, "Mother, may I?" He then must go all the way back to the starting point and begin over.

The point of our playful analogy is that when human nature by impatient willfulness withholds consent to the limits of the context of its progress, the eventual effect, if not the immediate effect, is that in some manner that "player" must begin over. Such is the "game" within the limits of being in respect to the discrete person's journey toward a perfection of potentialities. Of course the analogy is not apt in all its figurative correspondences. With the child who is "It" there is likely to occur favors beyond "luck" or "chance," as when personal relations of child to child affect the grace granted by the current "It." Protests of injustice, as any parent knows, are referred to higher authority beyond the limits of the game, the injustice argued in relation to the violations of the limits of the game.

Nevertheless, the analogy between contextual limits (of all creation on the one hand, of the limits of the current child's game on the other) as opposed to the differentiating particularities of conglomerate creatures (the things of creation on the one hand, the children in the game on the other) is very much to the point of our concern about "natural rights" and that concept's relation to "natural law." In both contexts, it follows that the participants—the things of nature, the children of the game—are limited in their desire by the limiting context. There is also the added aspect, made vivid by the Lord of grace in the game, the "It" who is omnipotent beyond the limits of the game to the point of being unjust or seemingly unjust. How much of our literature is thick with the concern. We need only mention John Donne's protesting sonnet on the point:

> If poisonous minerals, and if that tree
> Whose fruit [drew] death on else immortal us,
> If lecherous goats, if serpents envious
> Cannot be damned, alas, why should I be?

Such is the complex arena to intellectual concerns for the fairness—or unfairness—exhibited in the range of "natural rights" among the orders of creation. It is the intellect's address to that concern to which we now turn.

Natural rights, let us say, lie in the province of divine law if one attempts the concern from a Thomistic perspective. They do so in that those rights called "natural" are determined to man's intellectual perception by the nature of things in themselves, as divinely decreed by virtue of their cumulative particularities. That is, they are divinely maintained in their existential actualities. It is in this respect that "nature" may be understood as one mediator of divine truth to human intellect. But it must be understood at once that the *natural rights* of things—of lecherous goats or poisonous minerals no less than intellectual creatures—are determined by virtue of the limits of their specific natures. Therefore there can be no *a priori* granting of absolute judgment of natural rights by man as the resident Lord of creation, whereby he would lord it over "nature."

An effect of this culmination of particularities in limited creation—what we have spoken of as the *going-on-ness* of creation—in so far as intellect may perceive it is a tensional harmony-chaos. The perspective upon this tensional *going-on-ness* we characterize broadly as history, and from such historical perspective emerges the danger that intellect may lose its awareness of finite limit to its own perception. To lose the sense of limit in "historical" perspective is to suppose the perspective one of a visionary inclusiveness; we hold by intellect the whole of history. Thus history itself emerges as a pseudo-god of being, the danger in Hegel. That such is a truth about intellect's tendency to reductionism, assumed to be an opening vision of the whole, is sufficiently witnessed by social and political events in our century perpetrated by the disciples of Hegel and Marx. It is well to recall in this context, lest the larger concern of our argument seem too much to lose our putative concern for the Agrarian movement, that one of those Agrarians proposed as a title for *I'll Take My Stand*, "Tracts against Communism." That title was not sufficiently inclusive of the

V. Of Natural Rights and Natural Law: A Speculative Beginning

concerns, as we realize on remembering that the Agrarians were deeply concerned with the general manipulations of "nature," both human nature and the earth's body, by not only Communism but by a capitalism severely secularized. (We shall presently consider Allen Tate's address to this concern.)

"Mother Nature," mediating divine truth to intellect, reveals by that mediation the special calling of finite intellect in nature, of which it is itself a part. It is a part because it is a created being also. It is in this recognition that the limits of intellect's own rights in respect to creation is to be governed, through intellect's office in creation, the office proper to intellect's own "natural rights." That means at last that intellect's proper office is not that of Lord but of steward—a mediator among the diversity of those natural rights proper to the diversity of the existing creatures constituting the whole of creation. When intellect exercises that office with a right will, the person deports himself in creation with respect to and with respect for the peculiar nature of the discrete things in his range of stewardship, whether poisonous minerals or lecherous goats or endangered forests. Or family or business or agency. Thus the person's concern is properly for the potential order in nature through intellectual actions that are at last registered as "history," whether writ large or small. First of all is the necessity of ordering one's own peculiar "nature," and that is possible through intellect's understanding, within the gifts of its capacity for knowing its own being, the orders of nature as may be more largely taken. It is in this perspective that one discovers his calling: as lawyer, as governor, as father or mother. As gardener or bricklayer or architect or physician or priest.

And thus finite intellect, through its peculiar gifts, is enabled to make a proportionate encounter of the Cause of things through things in themselves. That is, finite intellect by the gifts of its nature encounters the essence of things, which to intellect in the effect of that encounter is that certain truths of things dwell in intellect itself. Such encounters occur within the complex of things, the whole of creation (including created intellect itself), out of which complex intellect derives the truth of things in themselves. Now one important aspect of this derived truth, in relation to the community of intellects, is what we call natural laws. That dimension of natural laws appropriate to the political and social order of the community of mankind is of such derivation.

We observe, however, that natural laws, though dependent within the province of divine laws, are subsidiary—are necessarily subordinate because we are necessarily uncomprehensive of divine law—by reason of the deriving agent's finite intellect itself. Nevertheless, given intellectual will as free, there is the tendency through will to elevate natural law toward an absoluteness, the accompanying error to the emerging presumption by willfulness that finite intellect is itself autonomous. At an extreme degree of this presumption, as in Positivism, one finds willful intellect establishing its own law as if an absolute. An irony to that presumption is the intention of such Positivist action to assume autonomous transcendence of natural rights by its arguments, but it does so on the principle of a relativism in creation itself as the underlying principle of existential reality. It is through this principle of relativism, we may observe, that the Positivist intellect would establish its own absoluteness as the operative and overriding principle justified by its own reductionism of the orders of natural creation through relativistic principles. Thus itself reduced by itself, intellect concludes its own transcendence, a most signal irony. The immanence of, but consequent self-transcendence of, intellect by its own operation is thus presumed contradictorily, since it is deduced from a relativism which cannot yield its opposite, the absoluteness of intellect.

In respect to the natural law determined from the province of natural rights, from the complexity of the existential reality of things in themselves in the totality of creation, we must insist always that natural law is derivative, whether natural law is to be related to social community or to acts upon material existence such as give rise to the intellectual disciplines of biology, physics or the like. Natural laws held by intellect as truths about existential reality are necessarily limited

V. Of Natural Rights and Natural Law: A Speculative Beginning

in relation to the recognized but not comprehended encompassing divine law. It is so in consequence of the limits of the agent exercising the derivation—namely finite intellect. As in all matters concerning the relation of finite intellect to Infinite Intellect, the relation of man created in the image of God by God to God Himself, the relation of proper proportionality in being as caused by Infinite Being, is the centering truth of the relationship, a truth adumbrated by St. Thomas in *On Being and Essence*.[5]

What the Thomistic Realist may observe is that, since the Renaissance, empirical science under the aegis of Enlightenment's rationalism issues in Positivistic science and philosophy. Positivism would enforce a positive law divorced from Thomas' natural law by an act of pseudo-transcendence of existential reality. What is lost is Thomas' location of the natural law: not law limited and derived from external nature (though made manifest in the particularities of things), but as an intellectual capacity to participation in creation—*with* yet *under* Divince Law. The participation is mediated to finite intellect through existential reality, creation in its particularities as experienced. The view is quite contrary to the Positivistic doctrine of natural law squeezed from material existence presumed a randomly deterministic accident, the derivative a power to be reimposed on existential reality by the ultimate authority of autonomous intellect.

Thomas to the contrary observes that man as intellectual creature "partakes of a share of providence, being provident both for itself and for others." Thus it bears a proportionate "share of the Eternal Reason, whereby it has a natural inclination to its proper act and end. *This participation of the eternal law in the rational creature is called natural law.*" (*Summa Theologica*, I–II, Q. 91, an. 2, my emphasis.) In this perspective, natural rights have implicit limit in the natures of created things, to be discovered by reason as ordering beings under eternal law. The sorting of natural rights to the benefit of creation is a responsibility of the rational creature in his deportment of stewardship through the complementary modes of his simple intellect, the *intellectus* (intuitive) and the *ratio* (rational).

VI

The Problem of Getting to Know *Natural Rights* from *Natural Law*

The terms *nature* and *history* have an intricate relation, bearing differing meanings in the history of our intellectual actions, so that here I must make clear once more my own sense of them. (I ought to say that my summary account is supported, I believe, by a great deal of the work I have done in a number of books.) In an initial sense, as I have suggested, *nature* designates the sum total of the particular natures of discretely existing things. It designates in this sense the totality of creation. But already involved is a corollary sense of the term which cannot be separated out at last, and which indeed is crucial to our understanding of the complexity implied in speaking of the totality of creation. If we are detached philosophers, this second sense of *nature* intends to designate the behavior of things in themselves, and here we mean of things in a range from the inanimate to the most sophisticated of animate things in the focus of our concern for the science of biology. Or that range of things from negative to positive matter in the intricacies of particle physics, if particle physics should be the focus of attention upon the nature of existence itself. In this second sense, nature as appropriate to the specificity of the discrete thing, I mean to designate the substance, the essence, the constitution of the particular thing—a sense of the term we recognize as out of Thomistic philosophy.

Given nature in this more specific sense, a term signifying the

VI. The Problem of Getting to Know Natural Rights from Natural Law

essence of the thing itself as designating an existing, discrete creature within the totality of nature, the necessity of intellect in its attention to such a thing is that intellect comes at last to discriminate among essence. Thus when things are recognized as distinct and particular things, there follows a necessity to intellect that it respond variously to differing things by attempting to understand the multiplicity of things. This involves our recognition of the orders of being, the orders of nature within its totality. But intellect can properly pursue an understanding of such order in creation only through a further, even antecedent, necessity to intellect. It must first, and in tandem to larger concerns for the orders of being, responsibly discriminate by understanding it own nature. The perfection of this understanding by intellect of its own existence as a created thing, a discrete person, lies in the discovery and development of the orders of virtue proper to intellect itself. That is a crucial necessity to intellect, and the one most generally neglected, as I may suggest by a further summary statement.

For intellect to refuse active responsibility to the orders of virtue proper to itself—a refusal always made by this particular person in response to his own existence—is to elect willfully to surrender to a pretense of understanding which ends in a sentimentality. Through this deportment of intellect one is likely to submit to nature in its several senses, but only through *feeling* as a substitute for rational and intuitive *thought* in concert. Bringing these modes to bear is a lifelong labor. The contrary deportment is a willful betrayal of the thing itself—first of all of the willful intellect itself and consequently of discrete things of creation other than itself, the things experienced by intellect. Most destructively, then, it is a self-betrayal. But it leads to a betrayal of the nature of things in themselves. What is involved is a denial of the very creatureliness of things (including the denying self) and thereby a denial in the end of the Cause of that creatureliness. This is to say, again cryptically, that the secularization of intellect we speak of as *modernism* is an effect, in its broadest present influence on community, of the sentimentalization of intellectual action in response to the complexity of nature. That circular effect isolates the intellect in a denial of God, trapping the discrete intellect in a closed, alienated condition of the self in nature which we may call self-love.

As we may observe all about us—whether in relation to agitated environmental concerns or political or social concerns in our recent history—this sentimentality (whereby feeling becomes the operative principle of intellectual action) becomes a substitute for orderly thought. The given intellect has a vague sense of responsibility for "doing" right and so feels good about itself when it acts on feelings. That is a species of self-righteousness such as makes intellectual discourse most difficult at this juncture of our communal encounters of nature. One may demonstrate the point at random from reading either the evening papers or the learned journals. What is denied by such deportment of intellect is a responsibility of intellect to its proper action, a responsibility for a *discrimination* of the orders of being under the governance of the orders of virtue, and in proportion to the limits of the divine law governing the whole of creation.

Such a willful if well-intentioned intellect becomes easily subjected to manipulation by more subtle intellects, those gnostic directors whom Eric Voegelin and others arraign in their writings. Those are the would-be lords of power over being itself, who through such power intend a radical destruction of the orders of nature made possible only through a distortion of the virtues of intellect itself. For that is the only means to such a deconstruction of being, a deconstruction of existential reality which must be effected first of all in subject intellects. They would become the mother of our will, to whom we plead, "Mother, may I." Surely, one needs little recall to remember how piously virtuous such programs have been made to appear in our time, from political left or right, in the attempted deployment of intellect as if in the interest of social community but with a concept of community distorted by utopian dreams. One need only name names. Stalin and Hitler are the most notorious, of course, because of their spectacularly destructive effects upon the body of creation. But one finds kindred spirit, East and West, wherever there is the

VI. *The Problem of Getting to Know* Natural Rights *from* Natural Law

righteous intent of power to achieve ends through a sentimentalized version of humanity. Solzhenitsyn, we remember, proved shocking to his Harvard audience some years ago when he suggested that the same gnostic intent of intellectual action underlies our Western as well as the Eastern manipulations of intellect by the intelligentsia, by those whom he speaks of elsewhere as the "smatterers."

With such words as these, we have moved our concern from that for the meaning of *nature* to the meaning of *history*. What I observe is that our intellectual concern for the nature of existing things in their particularities is a concern for the complex of effects among things out of their discrete natures. That introduces the concept of the *going-on-ness* of nature, which is the *history* of existential reality. For the gnostic intent is to usurp this *going-on-ness*. We say that *history* as a term is concerned with events in nature. In our most intense use of that term *history*, of course, it is centered on mankind's intellectual carrying-on in the world—his ancient, recent, present actions out of his given nature as an existing intellectual creature.

Given the rise of historiography to the status of a science since the 18th century, history becomes a term manipulative of existential reality, as we need only remember in relation to the appropriation of Hegelian thought through Marxist manipulations of thought to the destructions of nature—human and general nature. Francis Fukuyama has recently titillated the intellectual community by his restricted metaphor whereby he declares that we have reached "the end of history."[6] I myself rather prefer to put it that we have reached an impasse between two emerging communities of thought: the gnostic manipulators of nature through a history raised as if to a science and made thereby a limiting, a reductionist, weapon of intellect; and the reemerging common sense in the popular mind which is at last, at least in isolated places, overthrowing such manipulators. That popular mind moves restively and uncertainly and with contradictory actions, even as one moves physically when he wakes slowly from deep anesthesia. But it begins to move nevertheless. The gnostic manipulations of intellect are very aptly described figuratively as the anesthetization of intellect, and it is from this sleep that the popular spirit begins to stir, a stirring with great spectacle now in Eastern Europe and the former USSR, but also discernible even in the somnolent West.

Natural law as here understood, then, names a reality of creation giving rise to the complex question of natural rights in relation to community order, a subject of growing concern in the West. *Natural law* presently troubles our political debate. It is a term of disputed meanings in the arena of intellectual action. The dispute turns on the question of "natural" limits of intellect itself in its putative concern for accommodation to reality. But at issue always are the *natural rights* appropriate to discretely existing creatures by virtue of their natures within that complex: that is a pursuit of the limits implied by the finitudes of those discretely existing creatures constituting the totality of creation, and such a fundamental concept lies at the heart of our concern for political unrest in the "democratic" West.

There are limits discoverable in relation to the tensional engagement of this discrete entity to that discrete entity or entities in larger tensional conglomerates. In these encounters between essences in action, the discrete entity is properly ordered—that is, limited—within the purview of divine law, as opposed to the ordering effect of human positive law upon the community of persons. Here "nature" is understood to include both the nature of intellect itself as steward of existential creation, an agent of action in creation (through which action there occurs the community governed by human positive law), and the inclusive creation of the "whole" world, in relation to which intellect discovers its own particularity and limits as steward.

One might say in respect to the "natural rights" of this intellectual creature—the human person—that the term names a person's grace of limits, without which that person would not be or could not become that potentially, discretely existing creature, this person. It is in relation to this discretely existing nature (the person) that Aquinas distinguishes intellectual responsibility as morally related to the divine

VI. The Problem of Getting to Know Natural Rights from Natural Law

positive law, in a relation that is a continuing grace to existence itself (*Summa*, I–II, 91,4) and as politically related to human positive law in the ordering of the social and political actions of a community of persons. Thus St. Thomas suggests that human law can deal only with the actions of men in relation to each other and to creation in general and not with the moral grounds from which such actions derive their authority.

Human positive law cannot, then, have as its principal concern the virtue of the will in the individual citizen of a community, that virtue or failure of virtue which is the fundamental ground of action of the person in the world. It is in this inescapable breach between the limits of human positive law and the inclusive comprehensive infinitudes of divine positive law that one discovers the dilemma to human action in the world. Here lies the context of the drama of the quest for personhood. It is in this respect that we may understand how the discrete person may be said to do the right thing for the wrong reason or to do the wrong thing for the right reason. The ordering of the *doing* as a limit on the transgressions of other natures by the doing—in the political sphere, those transgressions of one person upon other persons or person—is the limited arena appropriate to natural law as it is given positive expression by intellect. We note in passing that a misunderstanding of this limit upon positive human law is conspicuous in the fundamentalist approaches to the problem, dramatized, for instance by the current Muslim fundamentalists in Iran and elsewhere which would assert an identity between natural and divine law.

The limits governing the existence—actual and potential—of the person is crucial to the validity of the term *natural rights* insofar as the principle so named is a justification of an intellectual action. It is in the discoveries of limit by the discrete intellect that it becomes concerned to do the right thing for the right reason, as opposed to alternative distortions occasioned by a confusion between the moral and political dimensions of human action. We have largely lost sight of the importance of the limits implied in the term *natural law*, limits inherent in the particularities of existential creation—the tensional complex of discretely finite things constituting the whole of nature. Thus the limitations as actual in that nature itself, under the providential grace of divine law, are not originated by intellect by its nominalistic uses of terms.

The term *natural law* is appropriated and used and abused by both the positivists, who adopt this nominalistic position on the question, and the would-be realist, who tends to confusions of thought in the question out of murky rationalizations of an otherwise valid position. The distortions by the would-be realist are occasioned by his imprecise reflection and articulation, as opposed to the intentional distortions by the positivist. Indeed, one might suspect that another, more accurate name for the would-be realist as here characterized is *idealist*. Further, a kinship exists between the idealist and positivist, but in respect to effected ends. Their difference is discovered in the intentionalities of the will of each as separate, as autonomous. As for this difference, the idealist sentimentalizes the positivist's end. In other words, both are utopian, the idealist "feeling" for the common good, the positivist rationalizing the common good as the justification of his gnostic deconstructions of beings to a commonality under the power of his own reconstituting intellect. A consequence of these sentimentalized and rationalized distortions is that in our time the terms *natural law* and its derivative *natural rights* are disjoined from their proper anchor in the reality of creation itself under the illusion that will is itself determinate of natural rights. The force of the will becomes the justification of the law of community. And this is an effect not only of positivistic intellects but of idealists as well, species of intellects not always easy to distinguish.

Little wonder, then, that the concept *natural law* has prescribed a public arena of quicksand to intellect—at the judicial, legislative, executive levels of our public concern. We have led ourselves to political confusions in our frantic attempts to escape the entrapment by our institutional concerns for the well-being of our nation as a political community. The problem surfaced in the early 1990s with sen-

VI. The Problem of Getting to Know Natural Rights *from* Natural Law

sational spectacle in the attempt to seat Robert Bork on the Supreme Court. It reached fever pitch in the hearings that led at last to the seating of Clarence Thomas in that body. These instances are here used emblematically to characterize our chaotic community mind.

There has been a rising agitation of debate over the term *natural law* in the wake of these hearings, simplified in the public media and engaged esoterically in great volume in the specialized periodicals. What we might recognize is that the issue has become politicized at this point and so not easily addressed philosophically. Once politicized, such a subject is reduced to confused address by diverse adversarial contenders who inevitably blur and confuse the truth underlying the subject of their concern. The subject ceases to be oriented by reality as it becomes an intellectual property of an advocate or his opponent, a property possessed by willfully abstracting it from the ground of reality in the interest of a current intent to political power by the abstracting will.

Once politicized, the issue when addressed in the interest of establishing its valid center will be most generally perceived as but one more adversarial attempt.[7] It is most difficult then to return the concern to its proper moorings in reality itself. What we have failed to do, in other words, is to respond to the necessity of determining *natural rights* in relation to *natural law* as governed by *divine law*. We have not said with a right and good intellectual will, "Mother, may I?" Instead, we submit to the worship of Progress as the Holy Spirit to the secular mind, a Spirit overriding by willful intentionality the limits in the orders of creation. The ultimate collapse becomes predictable. Intent upon shifting chimeric images of our dream Edens, we are thrown into confusions when the world in its realities kicks back. We are for a moment reduced to *ad hoc* attempts to recover intellectual orientation, even at points anticipating collapse, as suggested by our rising intellectual panic.

VII

Concerning the Impieties of Aberrant Will

In *I'll Take My Stand*, the Agrarians are scathing in their resistance to the modernist doctrine of "Progress" as promulgated under the auspices of applied science. They object that through that shibboleth civilization is being reduced by a dehumanizing industrialism whose end is a mindless consumerism. Thus John Crowe Ransom remarks that "Progress never defines its ultimate objective, but thrusts its victims at once into an infinite series." Such is the "gospel of Progress." Now if one takes Progress as the overriding principle of history, as modernist thought does, then this present moment—in the absence of next moment—must be accepted and celebrated as the most advanced point of all human history in nature. That is a position generally attractive to careless intellect, since it is pleasing to suppose ourselves in this latest of history's moments as superior to all other persons in all other moments as demonstrated by the things at our disposal. How could it be otherwise, since consumption has become "the grand end which justifies the evil of modern labor," as the "Statement of Principles" puts it. No age has been so richly consumptuous of the material world as ours. But the consequence has been that the "tempo of our labors communicates itself to our satisfactions, and these also become brutal and hurried." We labor that we may consume, the final end of labor reduced by the means to mere consumption until we find ourselves in a closed cage of our dehumanized "life."

VII. Concerning the Impieties of Aberrant Will

But here a caution in our opposing such a deracination of spirit by its dissipations of material existences: if we counter the presumptuous position of the gospel of Progress from the grounds of history only, as when we make comparative arguments concerning the present state of civilization in contrast to other points of past civilizations, it becomes difficult to withstand a counter, simplistic rejection of our argument. Our position is said to be founded in nostalgia, the ready charge being that we wish to "turn back the clock." An argument from past history against a present, progressivist version of history, when that argument has not sufficiently established *history* by a metaphysical understanding of its relation to nature, leaves our argument vulnerable to the undeniable ascendancy of this present moment of history. *Now* is always history's triumphant moment. Nor is it of much effect to underline the sad irony in those moments of "historical" certainty in the past, when we read in yellowed pages the triumphant declarations of a moment gained that will last a thousand years. In the ruins of the progressivist positions as held in the past, in the rise and fall of civilizations, their *now*, their present moment as history, seemed triumphant over any *then* as past history. We know now more than our fathers or grandfathers knew then. Even when in such a *now* we feel the sand shifting under us.

History alone, like nature alone, is no sufficient ground in which to build intellectual community. Today is history's salient point, more decisive as history than yesterday. The present will always seem triumphant when the only ground acceptable to our general understanding has been reduced to either today or yesterday. It is only as we begin to understand somewhat the enigmatic truth in the old assurance that "Sufficient unto the day is the evil thereof" that we may begin to move beyond those constrictions of history upon understanding that are inescapable in each moment, whereby the present swallows the past.

The constrictions are not ultimately decisive to our understanding of the truth of history and nature if we gain firmer ground for our recovery of both. We may gain an understanding of existence itself through a continuous moving beyond mere history, or mere nature, a move we always must make out of this present moment at the point of its conjunction with moments past. In that recovery we dimly anticipate the always emerging present moment, the moment dangerous to the soul's entrapment in the world. We must not become entrapped by necessity, by a self-willed determination of our intellectual journey as limited by moments past, present, or future. That is the consequence of any dependence on history alone to govern our journey. It is only by metaphysical vision focused upon event in nature as experienced by intellect—past, present or potential in the future—that one may escape the swamps of nature on the one hand or the bindings of thought by history on the other, in order to understand the truth of our peculiar role in nature and history as intellectual creatures existing always in the conditions *of* and *at* this present moment.

And so having made such warning, let us observe how the Agrarians' opposition to scientism relates to our argument concerning the relation of nature to history. In their "Statement of Principles," they urge a skepticism regarding the uses made of science by industry in advancing consumerism, a skepticism "even at the expense of the Cult of Science." At its base, their objection is not to science in itself but to the violation of the limits of science. Put another way, the objection is to the scientist's tendency to a violation of the limits of his own elected arena of history, whereby science tends toward gnostic alchemy. We ought to note here that the Agrarian objection is one already argued by G. K. Chesterton much earlier, especially in his *Orthodoxy* (1908) and *The Everlasting Man* (1925). Both the Agrarian objection to the abuses of science and Chesterton's old argument is that the scientist thereby abandons his proper deportment as scientist as he exhibits a species of intellectual action. The scientist may be accurately described as historian, even as prophet within his elected, restricted arena. Thus he responds to events in nature in a limited manner. Observed events lead him to postulates of commonality in observed phenomena, in events selectively considered. His

VII. Concerning the Impieties of Aberrant Will

concern is to formulate a theory about selected events in nature, in which respect he is "historian." And from his reflective attention to those events, anticipating subsequent events as a measure of his own observation, he corrects his historical evidence and his own reflection upon that evidence. He does so in relation to the accuracy or seeming accuracy of his past prophetic anticipation as measured by his immediate present experience of events anticipated.

Because of the arena within which the scientist as prophetic historian must restrict himself, the validity of his prophecy is enhanced. It is strengthened, we might say, by the strictures of limit. But what we have been plagued with since the 18th century at least, as the Fugitive-Agrarians came more and more to recognize, is a two-fold difficulty rising out of the more or less successful prophecies of science itself: first, the presumptive enlargement of the limited perspective toward universal solutions to the mystery of nature and history; second, an accompanying appropriation of the legitimate techniques of prophetic science to the uses of pseudo-science.

Thus develops an emulation of the legitimate prophetic scientist's techniques, appropriate to his limited arena—the techniques of the chemist, physicist, biologist, geologist, and so on—by those who would apply those techniques appropriate to the limited arena of nature-history to complexities of quite another dimension of nature-history. Thus rise, for instance, the so-called "soft" sciences, with their growing faith in an authority borrowed from the techniques of those "hard" sciences properly devoted to limited event. Here lies a failure to distinguish differences of complexity in the differing arenas of "scientific" concern. There rises, as an instance, that pseudo-scholastic Auguste Comte, from whom are descended anthropology and sociology. It is helpful to reread G. K. Chesterton's objections to anthropology as practiced, in his *Everlasting Man*, as well as the exposé of Comte's absurdities as scientist in Gerhart Niemeyer's *Between Nothingness and Paradise*.

When the appropriate techniques are misapplied in a larger and more ambiguous arena of event in nature, whether by the scientist himself or the pseudo-scientist, one might put the error metaphorically for emphasis: the techniques appropriate to the history of the atom in its participation in compounds is extended to the history of the person in his participation in community. We intend here a characterization by metaphor of the violations of reality through an abstractionism that ignores the limits of reality, that ignores the circumscribed intellectual arena which must define the appropriate techniques of particular sciences. This presumption upon false analogy effects a "softening" of science, improper as revealed by our metaphorical representation, since atoms and persons are inordinately parallel creatures as they are actually implicated in events in nature.

If we put the point this starkly by figurative excess, neither scientist nor pseudo-scientist will likely deny the violation in such a presumption that inordinates are ordinate. But the unfortunate truth about the prophetic historians of the soft sciences in particular is that they do not consequently reconsider the techniques required of them in relation to the complexity of event in nature. They rather enter an enlarged, and increasingly ambiguous, arena of intellectual concern as if guided by a true science appropriate to that enlarged arena. They atomize reality in the interest of an inclusive account of reality by intellect detached from its engulfing reality.

It is philosophy, not science nor pseudo-science, that must provide an understanding of the appropriate techniques that may properly orient the prophetic "historian," whatever his elected arena of intellectual concern. Philosophy will tell him if he will listen, for instance, that by the election of an arena there is the implicit presumption of both a context and limits prescribed by the realities of that context to the possibilities of his intellectual labors. Thus he may discover the appropriate limits to his finite intellect within the elected arena. For intellect must submit its exercise to appropriate techniques, whether dealing with particle physics or politics. Discovering, accepting and at last understanding these limits is the intellect's severest trial, since the intellectual person is inclined, by his will in support of his desire to know, to transcend the chosen arena, the arena appro-

VII. Concerning the Impieties of Aberrant Will

priate to his peculiar gifts. Thus he easily may come to think that he is exempted from the limits inherent in his gifts through the virtue of his actions. His own intellectual events he supposes make him independent of contextual realities.

Will, in support of intellectual desire, is a proper inclination, we must observe—one appropriate to the nature of man as intellectual creature. But it may dangerously incline the intellect to excess. For we must remember as most ancient the temptation to "be as the gods" in respect to our desired knowledge of creation and the causes of creation. The temptation was made persuasive to our first "modernist" intellectual, Eve. But wishing to be as the gods, very soon one wishes to be God, transcending good and evil (*pace* Nietzsche), those mysteries limited and embedded within the context of finite nature. The temptation then is to a presumption of transcendence of one's own finitudes by one's own intellect, whereby the infinite complexity of nature in relation to event in nature is subordinated to intellect's will to know. The next presumption is the exercise of power over all finitudes other than the exercising intellect. In this presumption, the intent, whether recognized or not, is to *exorcise* creation of being itself.

In dealing with the scientist as prophet on the one hand, and with the temptations rising out of his very success as prophet on the other, we are speaking of what we call in our day the virtues of specialization on the one hand and of violations of acceptable specializations on the other. The Agrarians remarked of the effects of transgressions of the mystery of nature and history through inordinate uses of specialization: we thus lose our "religion," they said. That is, religion "is the sense of our role as creatures within nature, a nature which is fairly inscrutable," as their "Preface" puts it. What is destroyed first of all is not nature in general, but our own humanity—our own nature as created persons. In the process, then, we "receive the illusion of having power over nature, and lose the sense of nature as something mysterious and contingent." These words from the Agrarians' "Statement of Principles" in 1930, let us observe, we encounter in a more rigorous philosophical explication of intellectual modernism in the work of Eric Voegelin, as for instance in his *Science, Politics & Gnosticism* (1968), as we find it in many thinkers concerned with the deconstructions of reality by modernism.

As any careful Agrarian or Voegelinean or Thomist would observe, it would be an error, in response to the abuses of intellectual specializations, to reject those intensely restricted intellectual labors because of the abuses. For the virtues of such intellectual actions may be properly ordered in response to appropriate finitudes of nature itself, including our own intellectual nature. Our virtues are ordered, we said, in response to the restrictions implicit in the intellect's elected arena of action. This is a crucial warning, given the present disintegration within the intellectual community, lest in our confusion we reject specialization altogether. Specialization allows a partial good to intellectual action which is not to be rejected. We hold to those virtues as limited, while recognizing that finite intellect is inclined to transgress its natural limits by its assumption of a power of transcendence over the limits of nature through its aberrant will. That is the inclination Voegelin speaks of as modern gnosticism, the desire for power over being. But the ordering of intellectual desire is not accomplished by rejecting desire.

We may not pretend to a transcendence of complex creation on the authority of specialization itself. That is the point at issue, requiring repeated emphasis because specialization assumes omnipotence since the triumph of rationalism out of the 18th century. The irony involved in this transgression is the implicit presumption of a transcendence over even the discrete, limited intellect itself by its will to power. There intrudes upon the intellect successful in its specialization the presumption that by its will it may lift itself out of finite creation, making itself thereby the god of finitudes. Such is the modern malady which Nietzsche so effectively dramatizes, the malady appropriated by Marxian machinations of reality that in this moment are everywhere collapsing about us.

In this light we might better appreciate the suggestion of one of

VII. Concerning the Impieties of Aberrant Will

the Agrarians that their 1930 volume be titled "Tracts against Communism," though the force at work against which they set themselves is more fundamental than that social-economic-political movement that plagues humanity in this age under the tutelage of Hegel and Marx. What we might better say is that the Agrarians opposed a deliberate impiety toward creation. That is why there is an added irony. For either failing to see this point, or seeing it and deliberately obscuring it, their adversaries raised spectacular arguments against them, depending upon ridicule. They are charged with wishing to "turn the clock backward," by those who would advance it against nature. Or they are said to wish to reestablish an agricultural nation like that in 1850. Their concerns were additionally characterized as limited to the local and provincial, to the antiquated "South." That was the terror of attack popularized and long continued, for instance, by that avowed New Southist, Ralph McGill. As editor of the influential Atlanta *Constitution*, he attacked them often in libelous columns, if intellectual principles are subject to libel through false words pretending to the truth of things. It little mattered that, in their "Statement of Principles," the Agrarians were at pains to counter this argument in advance, as a most cursory reading of those pages shows.

VIII

Loving the South, at a Growing Distance

The difficulty for the Agrarians in 1930 was that they intuitively recognized the dangers in modernism but were not intellectually prepared to oppose them. Rather, one might put it that they were not formally prepared to the degree necessary. In this respect they were somewhat like the Southern soldiery of 1861, called toward sophistications of battle out of their usual pursuits, in the Agrarians' case called (most of them) from their concerns as lyric poets and incipient fiction writers to a polemical strategy to delay the invasion by hostile ideologists who were increasingly ravenous to devour the human in the name of humanity. They had much to learn, and they learned quickly, but in the circumstances were in the awkward position of opposing the ideological invader with *ad hoc* defenses of truths intuitively accepted but not rationally entrenched in the popular mind they now set about defending.

Their adversaries, the modernists committed to the myth of progress through gnosis, recognized well enough how dangerous to that doctrine was the resistance by these articulate young poets and historians. But insofar as the Fugitive-Agrarians might be labeled as provincials, their resistance might be made to appear untenable, to be merely an obstructionist denying of the general good. Increasingly, the popular mind, north and south, was accepting the myth of progress, largely because it not only promised but was beginning to deliver attractive consumer things. As they put it in their "Statement

VIII. Loving the South, at a Growing Distance

of Principles," the growing appetite for "consumption, as the grand end which justifies the evil of modern labor" is exacerbated through technology, for there is more time "in which to consume, and many more products to be consumed." The "tempo of our labors communicates itself to our satisfactions." Thus the quality of life itself becomes "brutal and hurried," so that in the end "modern man has lost his sense of vocation." Vocation, divorced from its orientation as stewardship in respect to creation, becomes merely labor justifying the varieties of appetite that are celebrated as desirable ends of human existence.

The dangerous counterattack upon modernism by the Agrarians suggested the possibility of *provincialism* as a charge against it, to be made acceptable to the popular mind insofar as that mind had already succumbed to the temptations of the merely appetitive as the ultimate end of human existence. There lay ready an opening for such a caricature of the Agrarian opposition to progress. An older literary tradition of the South, it appeared, was an influence on the new literature emerging from the South which, once it had become academically respectable, would be termed the literature of the "Southern Renaissance." Simon Suggs, that broadly drawn frontiersman, himself given to appetitive human inclinations, would find new manifestations in Faulkner's fiction, a rich fiction safely encountered when held to the merely historical—a growth out of frontier humor. One could even handle well enough Faulkner's developing character Ratliff, the sewing machine salesman, as commentator on a slapstick world, on the outlandish world of the South. The spectacle of comedy bordering on farce allows one to ignore or subordinate the profound sense of human nature as fallen in that old traditional Biblical sense, though Faulkner did not. To engage the grotesque at the surface, at the level of spectacle, allows a conclusion that such fiction reflects the aberrant in relation to a restricted geographical location, an effect of a shallow response to inexorable history upon the South, now isolated and suspended in the backwash of history.

The more subtle indictment of the appetitive, as through the ironic humor of Faulkner's Ratliff, obscured by fictional events enlarged beyond history as farce or tragedy, may be the better accounted for in terms of mere history, as opposed to the complexity of human nature itself. And Faulkner's peculiar gifts in localizing his agents as believably native to his small postage stamp selection of the ambiguous "South" allowed a conclusion that his agents were indeed but local and not universal figurings of the human spirit tempted and fallen. They are comic grotesques, signifying a removed social milieux, and as comic therefore a satiric portrait of Southerners. That established perspective upon Southern literature would lead Flannery O'Connor, in relating her own fiction to the Southern tradition whose star at that moment was Faulkner, the Nobel Prize Winner, to comment on the "Southern writers, penchant for writing about freaks." That writer does so, because he still recognizes a freak, and recognizes as well that such may serve "as a figure for our essential displacement" and so therefore gains a depth for Southern literature. For, she argues, "our grotesque characters, comic though they may be, are not primarily so." They carry an "invisible burden," so that their "fanaticism is a reproach, not merely an eccentricity." If one asks of her, a reproach to whom? the answer is, to the modernist reconstructor of society, the gnostic mind which does not recognize how truly grotesque are those men in "grey-flannel suits," who are "even greater freaks" than those brought accusingly alive in Southern fiction.

Such, in brief, were the circumstantial conditions out of which the Agrarians attempted their *ad hoc* defense against modernist reductions of humanity. If in the sequel it was the fiction writer who more effectively resisted what Miss O'Connor calls the "dreary blight" of the "social sciences" on the attempt, the Agrarians in their resistance were themselves out of that literary tradition which led to Faulkner and Flannery O'Connor and Walker Percy and others. And it was they who could and did argue depths in that tradition, reaching deeply into Western history and not merely using an aberration of a locale isolated by history's backwash. Donald Davidson, for instance, became

VIII. Loving the South, at a Growing Distance

actively celebrative of the roots of Southern literature in ancient Greece and Rome, in both his prose and his poetry, particularly reminding us of how "Southern" are Homer and especially Virgil. From a certain perspective, of course, the Agrarians' sense of cultural origins seemed a mere clinging to broken fragments on the shores of time. This nostalgia as it was deemed, centered (in Ezra Pound's bitter summary of decayed cultural concerns) in "two gross of broken statues,/a few thousand battered books." So it appeared especially to the increasingly triumphant Marxism that began to invade American letters in the 1920s and appeared at last triumphant in the 1930s. Western civilization, "an old bitch gone in the teeth" (again, Ezra Pound), must be swept away in the rebuilding of a social Eden.

The "lost generation" of Fitzgerald and Hemingway and their expatriate associates—including Eliot and Pound—had reached a depressing end, leaving opportunity for the appropriation of literature itself to the progressivist ideology. Progress as a banner disguised from the popular mind the destructive reductionism which left humanity itself at risk, whether pursued by Marxism or by a capitalism divorced from the steadying governance of the ancient responsibility of stewardship. In standing against secular capitalism no less than communism, the Agrarians met local opposition from the emerging "New South" business community, and with recognitions paralleled by Pound's in London as reflected in his *Hugh Selwyn Mauberley*. In commerce no less than in cultural intent, the age demanded in drama the "accelerated grimace" and in sculpture a "mould in plaster" to entice the masses. One compares, here, Davidson's protest to the Nashville merchants who build their replica of the Greek Parthenon as a center of worship of the god of commercial progress. Even so, though at Nashville to local poets there seemed some strange aberrations, there was still some tolerance. For there yet survived for a little the residual sense of local tolerance, however much such tolerance was denied as existing from outside. If tolerance was reluctantly granted, still the poet was someone's cousin or son or nephew.

He might be tolerated even as one tolerated the eccentric uncle or one's mother's aunt gone in the head.

But in standing against the burgeoning left, with its Marxist agenda, the Agrarians irritated the usurpers of media power, largely established in the East—in New York City principally. It was from this quarter, in the next two or three decades, that the attempt to discredit the Agrarian position as provincial received effective impetus, and with an increasing success as the leftist literary establishment became entrenched in the academy, again principally in the Eastern academy. In discrediting the Agrarian position, ridicule more than fundamental argument carried the day, the trickle-down effects of which are still evident in the popular media's version of the "Southerner," as in television sitcoms.

It was the political and social antagonists of the Agrarians, those whose ultimate ends through gnosis was an imposed restructuring of humanity itself, who proved to be the provincials, as Allen Tate was to argue cogently at the end of World War II in his "The New Provincialism." In distinguishing the regionalist from the provincial, he put it: "Regionalism is limited in space but not in time. The provincial attitude is limited in time but not in space." For "provincialism is that state of mind in which regional men lose their origin in the past and its continuity into the present, and begin every day as if there had been no yesterday." It is the provincial who "sees in material welfare and legal justice the whole solution to the human problem."

As cogent as is Tate's distinction, we must realize also that in it there lies—as Tate recognized—the danger of its insufficiently accommodating the past to the present. Tate knew as early as 1930 a weakness of the *ad hoc* response to modernism in the Agrarian position. The weakness revealed itself in proportion to the dependence in the Agrarian argument upon history as the justification of a resistance. By the time of his essay "The New Provincialisms" (1945), he sees euphoria beginning to permeate the Western intellectual, an effect of the victory over Hitler. That is a grave threat to the regional spirit, an infection of intellect at a level deeper than any defense possible

VIII. Loving the South, at a Growing Distance

out of history or geography. Regional consciousness holds "honor, truth, imagination, human dignity, and limited acquisitiveness" as the justifying spirit of social order, requiring that defenses against modernism are to be recovered by metaphysical principles, if we are not to become "provincials who do not live anywhere," either north, south, east, or west on the world's body. Tate, in other words, is finding his intuitive reactions to modernism requiring a support by Thomistic realism.

He was thus prepared to receive the encouragement of Jacques Maritain, at about the time he wrote the "New Provincialism," and under the auspices of the Maritains as godparents he entered the Church in his fiftieth year. Such was his formal acknowledgment as it were of a solution to his growing restiveness about the inherent weakness in the Agrarian position. But he did not reject that position. He attempted to recover it to its proper ground. He never wavered in his belief that the ends intuitively recognized by many of the Agrarians were proper ends, but the intuitive truth only intuitively defended would not suffice. The provincial intellects who charged the Agrarians with nostalgia, with wanting to "turn back the clock," had too plausible a purchase in the argument when the defense was seemingly dependent only on history or geography or both.

John Crowe Ransom with his wry irony acknowledged something of the charge, a signal of his turning from the Agrarian position. In his "What Does the South Want?" (*Who Owns America?*), Ransom suggested that Southerners "are fully prepared to concede the bathtubs" and indoor plumbing. But such irony could hardly carry the day against the assault, and indeed Ransom himself had already given up the defense, as he would say privately on the publication day of his essay. He had moved a noticeable way himself toward accepting the New Provincialism. Tate's restiveness, his uncertainty of the ground proper to intellectual action in the pressing circumstances (in contrast to his certainty about the ends desired), is our concern here, in contrast to Ransom's changing position. Tate saw that the Agrarian position, if inadequately defined and defended in metaphysical grounds, would become submerged in intellectual contentions about history and nature as divorced from each other. It was a problem leading to disarray among the Agrarians.

We may pursue the point most economically, I believe, by relating Tate's disquiet to that growing disjunction from the Agrarian position Ransom was pursuing. Ransom would conclude that the ends he himself desired were quite other than Tate's. But the conclusions Ransom had come to by the time Tate entered the Church had been long since established in his thinking, even before the publication of *I'll Take My Stand*. He played out those conclusions more and more publicly in his discourse with Tate. Let us consider the proposition that Ransom was never so thoroughly an "Agrarian" as he appeared to be. And we may do so in relation to what we have just considered as the reductionist end practiced through science when science is commandeered by the modernist, gnostic ideologue. For by a misuse of science, specialization becomes raised to the authority of a metaphysical vision. That misapplication of science becomes possible when not challenged in metaphysical argument.

At the time Ransom wrote "Reconstructed but Unregenerate" for *I'll Take My Stand*, he was a vigorous champion of the position outlined in the "Statement of Principles" to that volume, of which he is the principal author. It was a commitment of his presence to the argument, a presence significantly absent from the tepid essay he contributed to *Who Owns America?* in 1936. Between those essays he was famous in the annals of the Agrarians for his defending the position in public debates, notably against Stringfellow Barr in Virginia. But from our late perspective upon his labors, we might be led to wonder at the degree of his actual commitment to those principles even at the outset. The enthusiasm, perhaps (so we might speculate), is to some extent a lingering effect of the lively speculative give and take among the Fugitives in the 1920s in their pursuit of the effective lyric poem.

Or one might wonder whether, in the sharp engagements following *I'll Take My Stand*, at which Ransom is effective by most reports,

VIII. Loving the South, at a Growing Distance

his deepest concerns in the issue, lying beneath his Agrarian arguments and centering in his concern for his proper calling as poet and critic, were not drawn steadily to the surface of his thought. Certainly, his commitment to Kant comes long before 1930, and the principles of Kantian philosophy are not easily reconciled to the Agrarian position. Or so I contend. I cite here words by that careful Thomistic realist, Etienne Gilson, made at the time Ransom was most active in his support of the Agrarian position. "[I]f the method chosen for pattern is that of physics, as was the case with Kant, metaphysics as a distinct form of knowledge becomes impossible, because the reason has been isolated from the understanding and deprived in advance of the sense of knowledge necessary to make it productive" (*Methodical Realism*, essays collected and published in 1990 by Christendom Press).

Gilson, in those essays written in the 1930s, was intent on distinguishing the philosophical realist from the idealist, and he stated rather clearly the realist position which Allen Tate was struggling to establish for himself in that period, even as Ransom was increasingly emerging as an idealist. "All idealism," said Gilson, "derives from Descartes, or from Kant, or from both together, and whatever distinguishing features a system may have, it is idealist to the extent that it makes knowing the condition of being." Thus the idealist, and the existentialist whom Ransom attacked from time to time, differ not only from the Gilsonian realist, but from each other. An old gentleman philosopher in a dustcoat trying the mystery of life from the pizza's quiet remove is unlikely to be tolerant of the position that *action*, rather than a thought managed by the fine instrumentalities of ironic detachment which are Ransom's, is outer evidence as well perhaps of that significant gift, intellect itself.

On the other hand, the realist insists against both that being is precedent and that an intellectual knowing of being is precedent to rational intellectual action. Thus Gilson's point was that "All realism implies an analysis of knowledge" which is already possessed by intellect, while "all idealism derives from the analysis of thought about ... knowledge." Knowledge as held by the idealist is held without a proper recognition that the knowledge is actually precedent to his thought. It is for that reason that idealism, locked upon thought as the justification of intellectual being itself, becomes isolated to itself. It becomes a disjoined little world of the self revolving on the axis of thought, and with the increasingly isolating energy of its own self-awareness. That was the terror at the heart of Eliot's early poetry. Ransom responded approvingly to that early poetry, as he would not to Eliot's poetry from *The Waste Land* onward.

It is to rational thought, to the gradual exclusion of intuitive thought, that Ransom would increasingly commit himself, and it is that inclination in him, present from the beginning, that would best explain many of his actions that were at variance with those of his old Fugitive-Agrarian friends, to their puzzlement or regret or even anger. Some of them if not disturbed were puzzled, for instance, by his move to Gambier, Ohio, where he founded the *Kenyon Review*. But what concerned him increasingly even before that move was the Cartesian-Kantian emphasis upon rational thought as the rescue of and justification of intellect to itself. Gilson put forth an objection which Tate was not yet prepared to articulate. The realist of Gilson's stripe objects that thought as an object locks one in his own intellect at last. That is why Gilson remarked of modern philosophy that the idealistic West becomes obsessed with epistemology—with the attempt to break out of the imprisoning restrictions by thought once thought is accepted as the initiating point of action for intellect.

The pathetic struggle of the idealist proves, again and again, to be his attempt to recover a relation of intellect to existential reality—to recover a comfort of intellect in communion with other intellects or with the things of nature themselves. Put another way, the struggle is to recover as justified an intuitive recognition that there is a precedent communal relation to actual things other than intellect itself, enjoyed by intellect before it attempts to certify its authority over experience through thought. That is the precedent relation whose effect is a knowledge in the intellect before thought intrudes. With the emphasis on thought as object, intellect isolates itself from the

VIII. Loving the South, at a Growing Distance

significant recognition that its knowledge is out of a communal experience between itself and things that is anterior to thought.

That anterior relation, indeed, is one to which Ransom paid tribute in his remarks on God and nature in the early Agrarian arguments. He advocated this acceptance as beyond any rational justification of the experiences of such communal relationship. The key term he used is *religion*, with which to name a phenomenon he saw as peculiar to the Southern character. In those early Agrarian essays, Ransom underlined the importance of Southern religion as based in nature. He did so in opposition to the severe rationalism which had given rise to a limiting science and through that science had established industrialism itself as the American way of life. He announced that the present threat was to eradicate that Southern religious deportment, the relation of the "Southerner" to adjacent nature. For Ransom found that deportment characteristically Southern. In his "Reconstructed but Unregenerate" he said: "Man is boastfully declared to be a natural scientist essentially, whose strength is capable of crushing and making over to his own desires the brute materiality which is nature; but in his infinite contention with the materiality he is really capitulating to it." And again, "The concept of Progress is the concept of man's increasing command, and eventually perfect command, over the forces of nature." Progress as a principle leads to "Service" as its handmaid and therefrom to various programs justified by such concepts as "Protestantism, Individualism, Democracy." Eric Voegelin, we note, spent a considerable gift of intellect exploring this very idea as pervasive of Western thought, and the purveyors of that idea he called modern gnostics, those who desire power ever being itself through *science*—i.e., through knowledge peculiarly held by intellect. We might easily find companionable words in the early work of Chesterton or the later-day essays and poetry of Eliot, concerned as both were with the sense of spiritual deracination effected by modernist thought. But in doing so, we would discover in these the decided inclination to orthodoxy which proves decidedly absent in Ransom.

When we have seen this aspect of Ransom's thought, which at the surface appears congenial to Chesterton or Eliot, we may well remind ourselves that the gnostic thought under attack is the child of Cartesian-Kantian idealism such as had already attached deeply to Ransom's thought. The issue of this modern species of gnosticism is practical science as now extended throughout the human community by a rapidly developing technology. That technology shadows us threateningly at the close of our century. Ransom can say with conviction that "A man can contemplate and explore, respect and love, an object as substantial as a farm or a native province. But he cannot contemplate nor explore, respect nor love, a mere turnover, such as an assemblage of 'natural resources,' a pile of money, a volume of produce, a market, a credit system." The Agrarian applauds his argument, knowing that industrialism intends translation of nature into intangibles. That can but mean "the dehumanization of ... life."

Alas, however, these gross effects which Ransom would have no part of are very much out of that rational thought championed by his patron Kant. The error as Ransom saw it in its contemporary manifestations of that thought was in the intentionality, not in the fundamental acceptance of rationality as the proper mode of intellect to the exclusion of the intuitive. In the end, Ransom's effective words about the proper relation of the farmer to his farm proved to be an analogy for his own increasing devotion of himself as poet and critic to the poem. In the end he cultivated the word as an end in itself, and one at least suspects that he envisioned the farmer as one contemplating the form as object instead of struggling to accommodate event to nature, his active exercise of a stewardship at each moment threatening to become a severe lordship. The objection that the Agrarians, with the exception of Lytle, lacked "hands on" experience of surviving in nature as farmers bears some validity, though a limited validity. (It is limited since valid knowledge is possible beyond the elemental muscles and sweat.)

One might, if he were Tate or Davidson in the early 1930s and even in the 1920s, wonder whether Ransom's vigorous support of

VIII. Loving the South, at a Growing Distance

Agrarianism might not warrant their own troubled analogy: Quinton Compson's insistent "I *don't* hate the South" in relation to what might be summed as Ransom's "I *do* love the South." For there was a certain philosophical ambiguity in Ransom all along, one which surfaced inescapably at last at the time of *Who Owns America?* It surfaced to the distress of Tate and Davidson and Cleanth Brooks. But it had already led to that earlier stormy break between Ransom and Tate, healed only by Davidson's brotherly mediation. Tate and Ransom fell out with each other over the value of Eliot's *Waste Land* as a poem. That early rupture of friendship between Tate and Ransom never fully healed, despite Davidson's good offices between them, and by the late 1930s there appeared to both Tate and Davidson a recognition that Ransom's heart had never been so fully committed to the Agrarian argument as they earlier supposed. Ransom's head had long since rejected the position for idealist reasons—reasons having to do with his separate and rather lonely intellectual detachment whose devotion turned him more and more to the poem as solace in that loneliness.

Ransom would be prepared in later years to acknowledge that poetic rhythm is a ritual acting "as a sort of substitute which had the advantage of seeming secular rather than religious, felt dimly but not sworn to" ("Theory of Poetic Form," in *A Symposium on Formalist Criticism*, 1965). In that symposium, Cleanth Brooks insisted to the contrary, against Ransom and Kenneth Burke, "literature is not a surrogate for religion." But from Ransom's position we can recognize the importance of this act as one of faith for him, not only to his practice as poet but especially to his practice as critic. From Ransom's position, criticism becomes a sort of substitute for theology, for the exercise of rational intellect in defense of poetry's ritual dimension. The absence of an apparent formal containment of that ritual in *The Waste Land* had been his grounds for dismissing Eliot's poem much earlier. It had also been grounds for his favorable praise of Eliot's earlier poetry. This is, incidentally, in ironic contrast to Davidson's own unhappiness with Eliot. Davidson's was not a concern for a formal failure in Eliot but with the seeming lack of a substantive commitment to reality on Eliot's part. Tate, of course, was left to oppose both, though he and Davidson did not reach the angry falling out over Eliot which occurred between Tate and Ransom.

Now Ransom's growing problem with Agrarianism lay in his sense that it lacked a philosophical grounding. It is the same fault Tate found with Agrarianism. But Ransom's increasing dissociation from the Agrarian position was in the direction of Cartesian-Kantian idealism, while Tate's is toward a Thomistic realism. His turning to St. Thomas under the encouragement of Jacques Maritain during World War II was its culmination. It is this difference between their choices of intellectual roads that concerns us. As for a belief in God as an existing reality, as the Cause of all nature, Ransom must be understood as at least agnostic, in which respect he is much closer to Robert Penn Warren among the principal Agrarians than to Davidson or Tate or Lytle. And that sets Ransom widely apart from the Chestertonians as well. Warren, in a tribute to Ransom soon after Ransom's death, delivered to the American Academy of Arts and Letters, remembered his old teacher and friend as "an ironist to whom irony was the only antidote for the tragedy of life." His conclusion was that Ransom valued "painful veracity more than self-indulgence and philosophical vision more than delusion." In these words, Warren summarized both his own and Ransom's skeptical defense against existence. Irony, we reflect, has been anciently the principle of intellectual survival in the face of the mystery of existence itself when intellect lacks metaphysical certitude, and especially this has proved so in our century.

Irony is in this respect a deportment exercised to establish a formal state of mind against the supposed chaos of the world. And it is significant that when Eliot abandoned irony for the hazards of paradox in *The Waste Land*, in an acknowledgment of the inadequacy of rational intellect to fathom the mystery of creation, Ransom began to find fault with Eliot as poet. As for Ransom's contribution to our letters in relation to Warren's farewell tribute, we recognize his as the

VIII. Loving the South, at a Growing Distance

deportment of a witty, ironic, analytical, playful intellect whose most serious concern was the order of words, and most especially the order of his own words. That is why we might find his "Pizza Piece" so poignant, in relation to words he spoke to an interviewer just before his death. He was, as poet and critic, "a gentleman in a dustcoat" trying. He tried by a detached irony, a waiting. But waiting for what? In that waiting, the poet prepares himself for an inevitable end, at which as he says late in life "he will be happy to subside, happy but used up, into the annihilation of death."

And so we may recall also that, near the end of his life, he once more described himself as a "Unitarian," as he had spoken of himself before. By that term he meant primarily that he was still, even as in his early youth and before ever encountering Kant, a "Kantian Transcendentalist." He meant by that phrase that by Kantian principles he was enabled to a possible rescue from Warren's "tragedy of life." That possible rescue lay in the formal, logical ordering of words. Such was, for Ransom, the salvation to intellect necessary against the disorderly universe, the mode of his waiting in the formal dustcoat of words, as it were, for his annihilation. Here one recalls that earlier in his career he had seemed rather indifferent to a companionable poet—that is, a poet who holds very much the same position which Ransom came to hold. I mean Wallace Stevens. At least Stevens held that position most of his life, though unlike Ransom, in the end Stevens entered the Roman Church. But it was only late in life that Ransom recognized his philosophical relation to Stevens. Stevens, too, was a formalist, finding his rescue for most of his life in the only acceptable "necessary angel," the imagination of the finite intellect as it manages the order of its words.

As for Ransom's position, one finds its rationalization, as Thomas Daniel Young pointed out in his biography, *Gentleman in a Dustcoat* (Louisiana State University Press, 1976), not simply in his post–World War II criticism but quite explicitly in those essays collected as *God without Thunder* in 1931, essays contemporary to his Agrarian "Preface" and to the essay he contributed to *I'll Take My Stand*. Those collected essays, indeed, belie the general tenor of Ransom's Agrarian stance against the encroachments of modernism upon the South. It is a position central to his famous arguments for the "Concrete Universal" in relation to poetry. The gist of his argument is not overly simplified if we say that he saw in artistic formalism the only grace possible to sustain intellect in a chaotic world, and it is a grace under the command of rational intellect itself, whereby one sets aside, except for the possible metaphorical play upon the idea, any thundering God such as Davidson or Tate or Lytle would insist upon. The God without thunder is the subtle Intellect in its ironic manipulation of words. Intellect justifies as universal its own actions through its uses of commandeered nature. That is, intellect establishes its own universe.

If we do not recover this background to Ransom's thought, we shall be considerably surprised to hear him, as editor of the *Kenyon Review*, extolling specialization. He had excoriated scientific specialization in *I'll Take My Stand* and, less aggressively, in his contribution to *Who Owns America?* But we have suggested he did so largely because of science's pragmatic ends which subvert society to consumerism, to a mindless appetite for things. That is a specialization quite different in its ends from that of Ransom's formalist criticism. Certainly in his *Kenyon Review* celebration of specialization, his was an unsettling argument to his erstwhile Agrarian companions who had appeared with him in *I'll Take My Stand* and *Who Owns America?*

We find Ransom in his "What Does the South Want?" (composed for *Who Owns America?*) hardly relating his argument to man's spiritual state, to the Southerner's spiritual concerns, as he had done in "Reconstructed but Unregenerate." This later essay, of course, is one concerned with Southern economic wants, but Tate and Davidson in their contributions left little doubt of the fundamental importance of the spiritual concern. The distancing that was at work between Ransom and those Agrarian principles was anchored in Ransom's more open acknowledgment of a growing discomfort with the traditional idea of the spiritual nature of man. His growing distance from Tate and Davidson was implicit in his last "Agrarian" essay for

VIII. Loving the South, at a Growing Distance

Who Owns America? But his old friends Tate and Davidson would have noted signs along the way, signaling their recognitions of Ransom's gradual dissociation from them. Their letters to each other reveal as much.

But even they must have been shocked when, as the distinguished editor of the *Kenyon Review*, Ransom engaged once more the old terms seemingly embraced by him in their earlier arguments, terms familiar to him since his childhood as the son of a Methodist minister: *sin, guilt, lost innocence*. In his *Kenyon Review* position, those terms are used with a flippancy close to ridicule. These terms in Christian doctrine are important realities of man's worldly condition, at least important to Tate and Davidson, but they became playful terms to Ransom, through which playfulness he rejected doctrine. His attitude to these Christian concepts is especially evident in his late "Postscript" to *The World's Body*. But even so, those terms were not used in the early 1930 edition of his book in the same way Tate or Davidson would use them. "See how long ago I abandoned that outmoded myth!" Or so Ransom seems to be suggesting in his late "Postscript" to *The World's Body*.

IX

The Specialization of Applied Prosody

If we explore for a moment Ransom's understanding of specialization, keeping in mind our own earlier insistence that science and its progeny, the multiple specializations of our age, are ultimately insufficient to the mystery of existence itself, we shall be better able to riddle Warren's eulogistic praise of Ransom's "philosophical vision" against "illusion." However, in doing so, we shall thereby call in question whether indeed Ransom's is a tenable philosophical vision.

In "What Does The South Want?" (*Who Owns America?*) Ransom's stance is that of an objective commentator, a mediator between the South and its requirements and the destructive expectations of it by the Eastern Establishment, Corporate Industry. His solutions to the South's needs, actually, are rather tepid summaries of programs already underway in the New Deal, and Franklin Delano Roosevelt is a more active presence than, say, Thomas Jefferson.

But more important than the line of political descent is the degree of presence of the author to his argument. There is little sense in the essay of Ransom's taking a position from within the community he ostensibly defends. Instead, he gives a cursory reflection on abstract categories: farmers, laborers, small business men, and it is quite evident that he feels little affinity to the persons intended by those categories. His witty irony serves him well here, less used in a rescue of the Southerness at risk than of himself from the burden of

IX. The Specialization of Applied Prosody

the Agrarian argument. He attacks the simplistic intellectuals who would advance either the cause of Big Business or subscribe to that growing socialist mentality which is advancing the cause of the laborer and farmer in an attempt to gain political power. Thus of the "Southern rural population," he says, "I believe they are fully prepared to concede the bathtubs" to the Progressivist approach to the "Southern" problem. As for the socialist agitators, "They have liked the thrilling odors from the armpits of men who work with their hands, and have admired the ox-like strength of laborers, and still more the ox-like herding together in comradeship, and in the gregariousness of simple creatures they have seen the sublime consummation of human society." How strange that they "have forgotten to make room for the most distinguishing of the human qualities, which is—intelligence." In that address, the speaker is safely removed from both the industrialist exploiters of labor and the socialist romanticizers of labor, leaving the speaking voice at a protected remove from both. But he is removed as well from the Southern laborers and farmers.

At the publication party celebrating *Who Owns America?* in the spring of 1936, Ransom confided to George Marion O'Donnell that he intended to write "no more economic essays." (O'Donnell gives us an account of their private conversation.) In September, Ransom wrote Tate that "*Patriotism* has nearly eaten me up and I've got to get out of it." Out of it to where? He added that the "modern artist needs an objective standard to replace that one supplied by the church for certain planes of experience." In the interest of a formalist, rational, logical standard, he and Tate ought to found an American Academy of Letters, thereby distancing themselves from the political involvements of "patriotism," which involvement cast them in the public mind as provincial Southerners. The founding principle of the proposed Academy: "to have our literature created by persons of philosophical capacity; to have its pure forms without taint or explicit philosophy." It is not an excessive parallel to recall here the similar position of a fictional poet, though one represented as considerably younger than Ransom was in 1936: Stephen Dedalus in Joyce's *Portrait of the Artist.* In addition, Stephen was intent upon founding his own academy of one, himself. For Stephen, the balancing of Ransom's two necessities to accomplish a "pure" form requires the omnipotent autonomy of the poet as God, who is also aloof from the final perfection of the poem and left "pruning his nails," indifferent to all other things in creation, including his own created poem. Ransom recognized, as well he might, that his now overt position "will seem to Don [Davidson] like treason and unfriendship." But "It's been on my conscience a long time," and so he must, in our recently popular phrase, come out of the closet and declare his species of aestheticism as the saving religion to intellect.

Remembering young Stephen as poet and the affinities of philosophical position between him and Ransom, let us recall as well another consideration. The principal Agrarians issued upon the scene largely out of their growing reputation as lyric poets. By and large it seems true that the life of lyric poetry depends upon the poet's uncertainty. He is moved to the lyric cry when stirred by an intuitive wonder toward or a perplexity about the nature of existence, and particularly about his own existence. From this point of view upon the tensional virtues in lyric poetry, a metaphysical vision becomes a handicap; it tends to erode the tensional intellectual energy that finds expression as lyric poetry. That is why, among other reasons, Dante's *Divine Comedy* stands as uniquely great. We might say of it that it dramatizes the journey of the lyric poet as protagonist toward a certitude beyond the limits of the lyrical mode. This most metaphysical of Western poems depends upon the metaphysical vision of its maker and it imitates by its action the lyric poet transformed to metaphysical poet. (To characterize the *Divine Comedy* as an *epic* seems hardly sufficient to its nature, for it is rather a metaphysical poem whose analogy in the tradition requires our calling it a combination of the *Works and Days*, the *Odyssey*, the *Aeneid*.) What is most impressive in Dante's accomplishment is his controlling his vision dramatically so that we have a wondering lyric journey whose end is a coincidence of the lyric poet as protagonist and the metaphysical poet as maker of that great poem.

IX. The Specialization of Applied Prosody

It is a commonplace in our observations about the Western tradition of poetry since Dante that progressively such an inclusive drama as *The Divine Comedy* is less and less possible, despite the many attempts by our poets at a grand poem. Pound, for instance, intended by his *Cantos* to do for poetry since Dante what Dante did in summary for poetry from Homer's time up to the 13th century. It is also a commonplace that the poets who follow after Dante seem increasingly committed to criticism, as once they might have turned to drama, as in Pereclean Athens or in Elizabethan England. They seem to find, at least in recent centuries, a necessity to rationalize their uncertainties as poets by a defense of poetry as a significant intellectual action. It is a rare instance when such a poet is by his formal or even informal preparation learned in philosophy. At least this is true since the English Romantics. (Eliot, the poet in contention between Ransom and Tate, was formally trained we remember.) Most often the lyric poet through his criticism stumbles upon the pressing necessity of a philosophy to support his attempt, led there again and again by the problem of epistemology. Thus Keats made an anxious request from his own retreat on Margate sands from London (repeated a century later by Eliot) for "three or four books" from which he might derive a metaphysics.

The lyric poet's deportment as philosopher, then, is very likely to bear evidence of the *ad hoc*. Little wonder that the lyric poet entering upon a social or political agenda will reveal a similar *ad hoc* aspect in his understanding of whatever philosophy underlies his polemics. He will most likely pick what seems useful in the moment's polemical pressure. And so we need not be surprised that the Agrarian principles as put together in *I'll Take My Stand* exhibit an *ad hoc* dimension to the principles these essayists advance. Their argument was made out of their intuitive recognition, from their experiences as lyric poets largely, of the need for a philosophical justification of the intended position. They grew, most of them, in rational defenses of their intended position, but it was an arduous struggle to do so. Tate's contribution to *I'll Take My Stand*, for instance, began with his encounter of the difficulty. He argued a necessity to start over as thinker, since it is difficult to "think for oneself." In order to do so, he stated it was necessary to begin with a "spirit of irreligion" in attempting to understand Southern religion, his elected subject. Of these Agrarian poets, then, it was Ransom and Tate who seemed most uneasy as to whether their position was adequately established in philosophical principles, recognizing a possible vulnerability to their polemics in consequence.

Robert Penn Warren attempted, and was impressive in attempting, the large dramatic poem, most notably his *Brother to Dragons*, but the remarkable point about Warren as poet was his recovery of his lyric mode in his later years. He did so through a sardonic irony which speaks out of an uncertainty, as in *You, Emperor*. But his was an irony distinct from Ransom's, which in contrast was so largely free of the sardonic, the self-accusatory, depending instead on the detached poet's setting a rational control upon a tensional balance in the irony. Thus Ransom made a dramatic, objective display of a lyric voice carefully dissociated from the poet, the maker of that voice. That is, Ransom, unlike Warren, was careful to exclude himself as a presence affecting the nature of the poem's irony, using the device of the masked voice to distance himself and additionally using the formalities of a highly sophisticated prosody to maintain that detachment. This point is not in deprecation of his poetry. It is a remarkable strategic success in Ransom's practice of it.[8] But our concern is not with the intrinsic virtues of the made thing, the poem, but rather with the philosophical position suggested of the poet, who becomes a polemicist of values to community but then comes at last to advance a polemics of his own independence from community. Such was the shifting of position for Ransom which would undoubtedly, as he feared, "seem to Don like treason and unfriendship," for such a dissociation is hardly acceptable to Davidson. Indeed, this is precisely the center of Davidson's quarrel with Eliot.

As formalist, as a detached poet of Ransom's sort, the poet's action is made ultimately in the interest of the poet himself, a justifying action by intellect of intellect. The significant universe is the

IX. The Specialization of Applied Prosody

one circumscribed by himself as maker and the poem as the thing made. But his intentional context of significant existence when seen from another perspective (that of Thomistic realism) will be declared a closed, isolated world. It is for this reason that Ransom by his actions, unlike Eliot or Tate or Davidson or Brooks as men of letters, helps prepare the academic mind to accept the dead end of Deconstructionism. He helped prepare that way in large part through his deportment as editor of the *Kenyon Review*. In respect to a commitment on philosophical grounds, beyond the concern for art, his position was presented as neutral. Or rather, he was publicly given to a philosophical pluralism. Where he was resolute was in his formalist concern for art as a making by the rational intellect, an art he saw as analogous to the specialization of the man of science. Little wonder, then, that he was often uncomfortable with his peers such as Eliot and Tate, and especially with Davidson and Brooks in respect to his philosophy of art. For they increasingly rejected Ransom's position as inadequate to the fulfillment of intellectual potential, most especially insofar as intellect is responsible to a community of mankind governed by a sense of proper stewardship of creation. That is the central "Agrarian" principle which Ransom distanced himself from. His was a position which his fellow Agrarians saw as a sort of stunting of intellect. It was a position suited to a minor effectiveness in one's making what Eliot might call minor poetry, in distinction from the *Divine Comedy*.

There has recently appeared in the *American Quarterly* a "Retrospective: Reviewing America: John Crowe Ransom's *Kenyon Review*," by Gordon Hunter. It is, alas, a rather superficial engagement of Ransom's position, one largely intent on rescuing Ransom as a "liberal." Thus Ransom, through the *Kenyon*, "successfully extended liberal values, though he had a "blindness—that today we would see as class-, race-, and gender-bound." But Ransom himself, in going to Kenyon College, told Vanderbilt's Edwin Mims that he must do so in order "to pursue the kind of writing which is peculiar or individual with me." That is a concern that commits him to no liberal agenda. The history of the *Kenyon Review* as an influence on our letters needs no repeating, and it is consequentially true that by Ransom's management it indeed served to advance Hunter's "liberal values." What we are rather interested in is Ransom's own philosophical position as distinct from political agenda, without denying that it established that influence, and with consequent effects quite antagonistic to the Agrarian concerns.

In the mid–1940s (as recalled to us by Young in his biography) Ransom summarized the argument of an essay in the *Kenyon* by W. P. Southard, "The Religious Poetry of Robert Penn Warren." In doing so, he associated himself with Southard's position. In summary, he says, "We are far gone in our habit of specialized labor, whether we work with our heads or our hands." Specialization had become "our second nature and nearly the only human nature that we can have." Now, in the mid–1940s (Ransom's approving summary), "Salvation is simple as picnics, or games.... but for superior sinners it must take a higher form, such as individual works of art, or religious exercises which are works of art institutionalized and rehearsed in ritual." Formal religion, then, is a species of art, with art the precedent and generic authority to religious practice.

Ransom chided Southard, however, for his proposal "to found an agrarian community within which innocence may be recovered." Ransom was comfortable in his reproach since such is a "fantasy" which he had himself "entertained ... as one of the Southern agrarians." Obviously, he did not want that old association held against him.[9] In defense of specialization, against Agrarian opposition, if something is lost, much is gained. "The pure though always divided knowledges, and the physical gadgets and commodities, constitute our science, and are the guilty fruits," but they are succulent fruits nevertheless. Commodities are, for instance, "clean and wholly at our service." And most important of all there is the specialization of art: "The arts are the expiations, but they are beautiful.... On these terms the generic human economy can operate, and they are the only terms practicable now."

IX. The Specialization of Applied Prosody

It was in his late "Postscript" to *The World's Body* (1968) that Ransom declared himself still at the end of his life to be "Unitarian," and his explication of the term is of importance to us if we are to see his reserve, his very ancient dissociation from Agrarianism, even as he argued for it. For, though very early on he recognized as a weakness in the Agrarian position its lack of a suitable and common philosophical vision, his own implicit and gradually emerging vision was quite unsuited to that of most of his fellows. It was unsuitable because it was questionable in its authority as philosophy, from the Agrarian position as held by Tate or Davidson or Lytle. It was, as Ransom candidly argued from at least the mid–1930s, derived from Kant, behind whom hovered Cartesian idealism, as Etienne Gilson has shown.[10] Ransom remembered having already "backslid from my father's faith ... before I came upon Kant the Transcendentalist," who became, once discovered, a mentor to his formalist concerns. Kant "did not dare make images of the Unknown God," and such too was the present (1960s) position of Christianity in general, he added, including "the Roman Catholic."

What is one to discover of value in Christianity, then, and especially in reference to Christ Himself? "Wherever Christ is mentioned, not as the great Saint or Prophet but as a junior member of the Godhead, it is because he promised to his followers that immortality which Kant had named as the third of three aspirations of the Pure Reason—the soul itself—even though it is the least capable of logical demonstration." The sophisticated clergy of the 1960s did not believe in Christ as God, but they were not free to "go about advertising their dissidence," since they had to "attend a service for the dead" and had to be socially considerate of the bereaved family.

Such has been the triumph of Kantian Transcendentalism, in Ransom's view, which therefore makes art the distributor of grace to the disoriented intellect. It is a position taking us back to Ransom's earlier article of faith in the concrete universal as the centering concern to art. That concrete universal is "any idea in the mind which proposes a little universe or organized working combination of parts," organized and made to work, we add, by the mind itself. There are two kinds of such universals, he argued, those of applied science and those of art. In science, as formalized by intellect, there is no "essential part missing, no unnecessary part showing." Those parts appropriate to formalized art are similar to the parts of applied science, in that the formal work does not attempt to satisfy an organic need because they are not located in the "animal perspective of human nature." They are pure and serenely detached from existential reality, as is true of the scientific universal itself. Each is a property, a commodity made by intellect through its specialization, for the use of intellect. One can hardly deny the compatibility of Ransom's position to that of Voegelin's secular gnostic whose intent is to a "power over being."

Ransom's is not a position compatible, then, to the Agrarian position of a Davidson or Tate or Lytle. Nor to the position established out of Thomism by Chesterton, that movement called Distributism, a movement Tate attempted to join to the Agrarian movement through the symposium, *Who Owns America?* Concerned with Tate as ally toward the possible establishment of his "American Academy of Letters," Ransom participated though he was so "eaten up" by such "patriotism," as he told Tate, that he must "get out of it." If one wishes to discover the cause of a continuing disquiet with Ransom on the part of his old fellow artists in the Agrarian movement, his contemporary colleagues in the cultural wars, it lies precisely here, and it is an aspect as well of their less marked but cautionary distance from Robert Penn Warren, who was more clearly of Ransom's party than of theirs. Davidson's and Tate's letters will reveal as much. What we underline here is that Ransom, recognizing the necessity of a philosophical position to an effective address to nature and society, established one which is quite inadequate to the position implied by the "Statement of Principles" he helped compose for *I'll Take My Stand* and his own essay in that symposium. Tate, recognizing the same problem, and indeed in some degree recognizing Ransom's position as exacerbating the problem, moved in a quite different

IX. The Specialization of Applied Prosody

direction to recover his own philosophical vision. He moved uncertainly toward Orthodoxy until he met Jacques Maritain at Princeton during World War II. Under Maritain's guidance, he moved more steadily in that direction up to his fiftieth year. In December of 1950, with Jacques and Raissa Maritain as his godparents, he entered the Church.

Angelism and the Poet's Made World

In December of 1949, a year before he entered the Roman Church, Tate wrote Wallace Stevens in response to Stevens' suite of ten poems in *Poetry Magazine*, "Things of August." He singled out the second and third as "stating differences" between himself and Stevens. The differences lay in their differing philosophical visions. Tate remembered his old and continuing admiration of Stevens' "Sunday Morning," and would pay tribute to that poem and to "Things of August" as poems such as he was incapable of writing because of what he represented in his letter as a limit in himself. In truth, however, he saw a limit in the philosophical implications and assumptions by Stevens as distinguished from his own position, his realism as opposed to Stevens's idealism. He could never reach that "*angelisme* of the intelligence which defines horizons that neither love nor hate," he said, quoting Poem II of Stevens' sequence.

Stevens, arguing for his sort of stillpoint as effected by imagination's words, speaks the idealist's case for intellect. But, said Tate, "The man who breathes the air of the well [an allusion to Poem II once more] cannot breathe purer air unless it be the air of revelation: the angelic intellect is not within his reach." Stevens' poems, then, are "a new way of putting ... *the* dilemma" of our time: "either the revealed access to the world [through grace] or the angelic mind looking down upon it" (Quoted in Radcliffe Squires, *Allen Tate: A Literary Biography*, 202).

X. Angelism and the Poet's Made World

Tate, admiring the tonal serenity of Stevens' poems, recognized of course the dangers of the angelic intellect as embraced by Stevens, having learned those dangers at least from Jacques Maritain, though already having experienced them as a temptation to himself over the years. It is the temptation whose liberty is (to quote Stevens' Poem II) that of "the air of the grave," though in his serenity Stevens insists it is otherwise. For Stevens, it is a "native" freedom which is within "the space of horizons that neither love nor hate." Those horizons are defined by his intellectual assertion, as in this poem's opening words: "We make, although inside an egg,/ Variations on the words spread sail," the words sailing within the asserted limits of the horizon of that egg, the head itself. The limits of the universe as so decreed by intellect are the limits of this discrete human skull, in this instance the one named Wallace Stevens. By assertion Stevens concludes the intelligence to have created "its true solitude" and it does so "in what it says,/ The peach of the last intelligence" (Poem II). (At the time of Stevens' poem the epithet "egg-head" was becoming a popular canard to aim at intellectuals, especially intellectual politicians like Adlai Stevenson. Likely, the poet expects our recognition of his whimsical wit, a characteristic playfulness in his poetry.)

It may be, in another perspective (Stevens continues) "the same thing without desire." That is, it may be the illusion that "in this intelligence" one mistakes the enclosed terrarium of intellect within the egg "for a world of objects," as if there were indeed actual things thus contained within the limiting horizons of this egg of the self, made so contained by its act of a structured world. As creator it makes this actuality of words, the poem, as God makes that egg of intellect if seen by analogy from the Thomistic view of *person*. It does so for Stevens, however, by an assumption of godhead, by *angelism*. Thus as maker, the poet is moved by "neither love nor hate." Such is the condition possible to the angelic intelligence, looking down upon its self-containing and contained universe. What seemed to impress Tate was the sense of serenity through what must be declared an angelically autonomous, and so a heretical, intellect. He observed, however, from his own developing Thomistic position, and so he had to conclude that Stevens embraced an illusional state of mind.

Of course, Stevens' artistic effect of serenity was not so deeply established as the art proposes, as we must realize when we discover him at the end of his life acknowledging that inadequacy. In his last days he requested baptism and entry into the Church, as Tate had earlier done. That is a biographical event still puzzling and disappointing to some devotees of Stevens's poetry. But Tate had already recognized the inadequacy of that self-isolating idealism, before Stevens came to openly acknowledge it. It had been a thematic thread in his own poetry all along, one which allowed him little abiding comfort. Whatever one may say of Tate's poetry by comparison, serenity is not one of its notable virtues. Still, he recognized a virtue in Stevens's made things as made things, a quite separate question from the poet's spiritual content, as St. Thomas said most resolutely.

If Stevens in "the quiet middle of the night" could appear content with "the broken statues standing on the shore," as his poem says, Tate could not, and he would as well have recognized in such images an echo of that other poet who could not either—Eliot, who found such statues of art to be "heaps of broken images." Or again, they are "withered stumps of time" that are insufficient consolation, though ever so beautiful. Tate, too, had sat upon the shore, with such fragments as he too had attempted to shore against his own ruins, to recall the conclusion of *The Waste Land*. His "Ode to the Confederate Dead" dramatizes that old sense of the inadequacy of art alone, as Eliot had discovered about art as salvific before him.

Tate, as perceptive as he was to nuances in such sophisticated poets as Stevens, then, would have engaged as well that seeming serenity in the modern poet he admired most of all from his first encounter, T. S. Eliot, and this long before his letter to Stevens in 1949. The illusion of serenity in Eliot's early essays is counter to the disturbed consciousness in the early poetry itself and required close scrutiny. There is the famous essay of 1919, "Tradition and the Individual Talent," in which Eliot divided himself as critic from himself as poet. He was

X. Angelism and the Poet's Made World

specific in rejecting in the essay the traditional Thomistic definition of the *person*. Indeed, he exercised in that essay a deportment of intellect very like that advocated by Wallace Stevens, who insisted on the primacy of intellect as governed by its "necessary angel," the imagination. That was for Stevens, as it became for Ransom, the only possible rescue of intellect from the chaos of personal encounters with reality. Eliot's early stance, too, was angelic, a dimension of his influential early essays insufficiently considered for the most part. Eliot as critic at that point was the detached mind looking down upon itself.

By this strategy of a dualism engineered by intellect, Eliot would deny the "essential unity of the soul," as he said. By that strategy as exercised from his angelic detachment, he accepted intellect in its act of making (whether making the poem or the essay) as superior to the *person* who constitutes the locus of the intellectual action, in relation to which historical and bodily presence the making occurs. The poet or critic, by the act of detachment from himself as person, is separate from the actual person inhabiting the environs of London, T. S. Eliot. That he would at last seem to himself a disembodied consciousness, plagued by the same terrors that assail his disembodied consciousness named Tieresias in *The Waste Land*, lay just ahead for him. For the moment, however, his *person* was a gathering locus for "personal" images and ideas, accumulated largely through the senses for disposal by the angelic intellect in Stevens's "words spread sail."

With this fund of images, the angelic intellect would, to borrow a figure for the process from Wallace Stevens, make those horizons suited to intellect, thus building the world of a fictional egg. It is a world closed by will, and its parts are the images as ordered by the imagination. We should not overlook a point: Eliot's formal deportment as rhetor in the essays of his early period intended a removal of himself as person from his arguments no less than he intended by his adoption of masks of personae in the poems. More is at issue, it turns out, than the art of the essay or the poem. When Eliot came at last to recognize that indeed the issue was larger, he did so through a traumatic revolt of the "person" he was. The significant witness of that revolt is *The Waste Land*, the poem that proved so unsettling to John Crowe Ransom, who had been a champion of Eliot's earlier poetry.

There is a centrally important confession from the detached persona of the essay "Tradition and the Individual Talent": "The point of view I am struggling to attack is perhaps related to the metaphysical theory of the substantial unity of the soul: for my meaning is, that the poet has, not a 'personality' to express, but a particular medium ... in which impressions and experiences combine in peculiar and unexpected ways." By his rejection of the orthodox belief in the substantial unity of the soul, Eliot allowed himself to build into his essay a dangerous dualism, one which reduces intellect from its experiences of substantive being, held as *truth* by intellect, Thomas says, to become merely a repository of those experiences which by will are declared convenient to the angelic maker, the poet. By angelic transcendence of himself as person, the poet escapes that ambiguous term *personality*, a term much labored in the 1920s, especially with the advent of Freudian and Jungian psychologies.

In his *Creative Intuition and Poetic Knowledge* (1953), Jacques Maritain looked at Eliot's "The Perfect Critic" (1920) and "Tradition and the Individual Talent" (1919) and found the argument confused. Maritain's objection is useful to us in that, coming relatively late, he was engaging the continuing influence of those early Eliot essays, centered in the academy, on our criticism of those early Eliot essays. From those arguments Eliot had himself attempted to distance himself in the interval. And in that interval it had been Maritain who exercised an influence on Eliot as essayist and poet, specifically bringing to his attention the validity of the doctrine of the essential unity of the soul. That is the doctrine central to Maritain's very influential little book, *Art and Scholasticism*, published in 1920. Its first publication is contemporary to Eliot's early angelic essays, though Eliot seemed not to respond to that work for a decade. Eliot would have occasion to look more closely at Maritain's argument after 1930, citing it in support of his own changed position, as we shall see. After *The Waste Land*,

X. Angelism and the Poet's Made World

Maritain would also become an increasing influence on Tate as well. For this reason, what Maritain had to say about Eliot's early essays is helpful to us in understanding not only the later Eliot but Eliot's young disciple on their common journey, Allen Tate.

"Emotion," said Maritain in his *Creative Intuition in Art and Poetry* (1953), "does not know: the intellect knows.... It is not emotion expressed or depicted by the poet, an emotion as a *thing* which serves as a kind of matter or material in the making of the work, nor is it a thrill in the poet which the poem will 'send down the spine' of the reader." Maritain insisted that the issue hinged on Thomistic intentionality, on a making which is the fulfillment of the potentials of *person* as a creature created with a capacity to know intellectually. Little wonder, then, that in an extended note to this passage we find Maritain charging Eliot directly with "serious equivocation," because he overlooks this distinction. Eliot's argument relative to the poet's use of emotion centers in "brute or merely subjective emotion," which we ourselves (separate from Maritain) are suggesting here to be a reductionism at the expense of the *person* of the poet. Person thus is made the matter out of which the poet by his transcendence of himself would make his poem. That Eliot was somewhat aware of this characterization of his detached position is reflected in his celebration of the poet as martyr to his poem in that early essay: "The progress of an artist is a continual extinction of personality."

Much later, in his Charles Eliot Norton lectures at Harvard (1932–33), *The Uses of Poetry and the Uses of Criticism*, Eliot gave his final lecture under the title "The Modern Mind." In it he summoned Maritain's *Art and Scholasticism* to the support of his own position at that later time, and against Matthew Arnold's high expectations of poetry as man's means of salvation. He quoted Maritain: "It is a deadly error to expect poetry to provide the super-substantial nourishment of man." And near the end of his lecture, he summoned Maritain once more to make clearer his own emerging position, now more radically changed from those early essays than he would admit in the opening Page-Barbour Lecture which he was to give that same year at the University of Virginia, published as *After Strange Gods*. Though his sophisticated Harvard audience was not likely to accept Maritain's insistence that, as Eliot put it, the "unconcealed and palpable influence of the devil on an important part of contemporary literature ... is one of the significant phenomena of the history of our time," another observation by Maritain, said Eliot, "may be less unacceptable": "By showing us where moral truth and the genuine supernatural are situated, religion saves poetry from the absurdity of believing itself destined to transform ethics and life: saves it from overweening arrogance."

Maritain in this statement was attacking the Joyce-Dedalus concept of the uses of poetry as the rescue of intellect from its entrapment by the sordidness of reality. That was the position which Wallace Stevens and John Crowe Ransom embraced, as Eliot had at first attempted to do. It was the position Eliot had embraced, only to discover it an illusion. Now at the new *personal* level of 1930 he prepared himself to accept that an overweening arrogance of intellect makes intellect the ready agent to the machinations of the devil in some modern literature, including some of his own. Nevertheless, he was careful not to say as much to the sophisticated, largely modernist, Harvard audience. By 1930 Eliot was prepared to believe, as did Baudelaire, that the devil's cleverest wile to the modern mind is to convince that mind that the devil does not exist. Donald Davidson, we have suggested, rather thinks *The Waste Land* a prime illustration of Maritain's point, so that we might from Maritain's, and from Eliot's perspective by 1930, be rather inclined to see Ransom's position on the poem as more cogent than Davidson's. This is a suggestion requiring some elucidation.

What was dangerous to the intellectual community of the day in that poem was the emergence of Eliot's growing recognition that poetry is insufficient to the rescue of intellect. The tensional poles in the poem are between the attempt of a residual—a younger—Eliot to maintain his old position on the one hand, and his growing recognition of art's insufficiency as savior of intellect on the other. That

X. Angelism and the Poet's Made World

gnawing subversive truth would no longer be denied. The struggle for form in reconciling the dying youthful desire for autonomy and the insistent truth that such a position is illusional, if supposed salvific, will explain I believe the dimensions of what might be termed paradoxically a formal cacophony in the poem. The orderly disorder in the poem is within the poem's surface spectacle of disorder. The spectacle makes it engaging beyond being merely an expression of the "personality" of the poet, who at the time of its composition is undergoing a spiritual crisis. It is in the end a poem dramatizing the tensional context which is always present to intellectual man in his pursuit of that which may at last satisfy his desire for a rest beyond tensional lesions in the soul.

In this respect, though Ransom was in some degree right in calling attention to the formal difficulties of the poem, his criticism that so angered Tate in 1923 was in the end superficial since it never got beneath the poem's spectacle. They are so, not in that Ransom was wrong in his analytical descriptiveness of the poem in respect to its surfaces, but that he did not see in what way the surface disjunctions reflect, through art's control, the reality of that deeper consciousness which Eliot would characterize in his Norton lectures as "the modern mind," a mind wandering and deracinated. It is a mind which for all its sophistication has lost the guidance of reality to its journey through the world. Consequently that mind cannot adjust to existential reality.

Ransom remarked in the review that so offended Tate that Eliot's fragments were "at different stages of fertilization," some of which were "emotions recollected in tranquility and others are emotions kept raw and bleeding." But that observation will not be a sufficient ground to conclude that on "not a single occasion" in the poem can one find "where his context is as mature as the quotation which he inserts into it." When Tate reacted in anger, he reacted, not to Ransom's argument, but to its high-handed dismissive tone, such a tone incidentally to which many subsequent critics object. But ironically, it is also the high-handed dismissive tone that we find in Eliot's own early criticism. Having prepared by his observations to recognize something of why Eliot's poem is so variously disturbing to the intellectual community, Ransom by his dismissive tone feels content to come to rest on the mechanics of form. Because *The Waste Land* "presents meters so varied and such a load of grammar and punctuation and such a bewildering array of discrete themes," Ransom would not grant that it is "*a* poem."[11]

The high-toned, magisterial detachment of the speaker in Eliot's famous early essay is belied by the dissolving selves in Eliot's other surrogates, in Prufrock and Gerontion and so on. As early as his "Preludes," he had caught and been mortally infected by that dissolving terror incipient in Stevens' own projected serenity of an egg-world presided over by the angelic intellect. For Eliot's intellect as early as 1910 found itself enriched only by the "thousand sordid images/ Of which [its] soul was constituted." Those images flicker against its horizon, the tenement house "ceiling," even as new sense images stir terrors. Images speak a threatening world other than intellect. The terror grows, since the intellect's own "vision" of that world is one which that other, the outer, world "hardly understands." One comes, then, out of the various dissolving personae of Eliot's early poetry, to that deracinated voice of *The Waste Land*. It is a self, a consciousness, which willy-nilly finds itself at large in that larger world. Thus Eliot's pivotal poem, *The Waste Land*, is a reflection of the spiritual crisis in Eliot himself, a crisis which modernism more comfortably speaks of as a "nervous breakdown," having rejected any possibility of spirit.

Here we recall once more Ransom's own high-toned words in "Reconstructed but Not Regenerate," his contribution to *I'll Take My Stand*: "Deracination in our Western life is the strange discipline which individuals turn upon themselves, enticed by the blandishments of such fine words as Progressive, Liberal, and Forward-looking." Ransom in this essay was attacking the activist political and commercial community, but he characterized accurately the inevitable spiritual deracination out of Cartesian idealism which turns intellect upon itself. And that is the crux of Davidson's early quarrel with

X. Angelism and the Poet's Made World

Eliot, as opposed to Ransom's quarrel with the formalistic, with formulae of structure, as the failure of Eliot's *Waste Land*.

Given Ransom's subsequent public expressions of his own intellectual isolation as the only possible defense against the chaos of the existential world, one almost suspects a faintly sardonic note in his characterization of this as "*the* dilemma" of the modernist intellect. One has such a suspicion, at least, when he recognizes that, as we have already indicated of Ransom's position, Ransom's central quarrel with modernism hinged at last less on its intellectual position than on its uses of that position for lesser ends in the affairs of man—the modernist commitment to consumerism, for instance. For Ransom was himself, as was Stevens, given to making "inside an egg,/ Variations on the words spread sail."

Ransom might well have embraced Stevens's conclusion to Poem IX of "Things of August." "It is a text that we shall be needing," Stevens says,

> A text of intelligent men
> At the center of the unintelligible,
> As in a hermitage, for us to think,
> Writing and reading the rigid inscription.

Such a deportment of the intellect as angelic, as the autonomous maker of texts which will suffice for a moment's serenity, was insufficient to Tate, as it was all along to Davidson and at last to Eliot. Tate, having sat upon those shores toying with heaps of broken images, could only conclude that the serenity of Stevens or Ransom is a serenity rested in illusion, making more evident "the dilemma" of modernist idealism out of Descartes and Kant. He had long since come to himself as in a dark wood, before his 1949 letter to Stevens. But it had not been easy to recover the path in those woods. Indeed, it was a year later than his letter to Wallace Stevens that Tate, when he was fifty years old and therefore not in the middle of his life, entered the Church. At that time, the Maritains were translating Tate's "Ode to the Confederate Dead" into French, in celebration perhaps of the resolution of the tensional conflicts in that poem. But that was well in Tate's future as he undertook the gathering of essays by the Chestertonian Distributists and the Southern Agrarians, published as *Who Owns America?*

XI

Ownership vs. Stewardship: Signposts at the Parting of Ways

If Ransom's contribution to *Who Owns America?* is disappointing, so too is Tate's. Indeed, Tate was disappointed with his essay before the book ever appeared. He wrote Davidson (January 18, 1936): "I have no alibi for my article. It is simply that the technical subject of property was beyond me, and I ought to have had sense enough not to take it on." What is confusing in the piece, separate from technical questions of property as addressed by statutes, is the inadequacy of the philosophical ground in Tate's attempt. It is a ground which he is nevertheless struggling to come to, the struggle evident in the essay. For that reason, let's look at a few preliminaries about that essay as it might relate to Tate's polemical position before and after it, and to his concern for establishing philosophical grounds.

In "Notes on Liberty and Property," Tate's thesis is summarized in his conclusion: "Ownership *and* control are property. Ownership without control is slavery because control without ownership [as by a corporation] is tyranny." When he posits effective ownership at the outset (i.e., ownership *and* control), he declares that "It is not a metaphysical essence. Unlike liberty, it is not a thing of the spirit." Rather it is an active ownership of existing things—land, a store, a factory. But, we might object, if not in itself a "metaphysical essence," ownership is inescapably out of a metaphysical essence, namely that little world, the owner himself, and in failing to make such a relationship clear, Tate must wrestle increasingly with the nature of the problem of *effective* versus *ineffective* ownership. Ownership, or so Tate might well have chosen to put it by 1950, is of existing *things* by a discrete *person* and consequently is a spiritual office dependent in the metaphysical essence of that person who is the designated and legal owner. That office must be oriented by the will of intellect, and it must be exercised in relation to the metaphysical essences of the owned thing or things. For if one is to use such a term as *metaphysics*, in its traditional sense as understood by orthodoxy, each discrete thing, by virtue of its being a discrete thing, has an essential nature, without which it would not be the thing it is. We make the point here, because Tate in the 1930s was certainly seeking an orthodox position through which he could orient himself to existential reality. His contribution to *I'll Take My Stand* was ripe with his concern.

What is at issue in respect to a metaphysical ordering of intellect in relation to existence in general, and so specifically to the spiritual relation of intellect to its own property, is stewardship. The buried point, never adequately exhumed, is in the difference between Tate's two kinds of property addressed in his "Notes." The difference between "real private property" and collectivist ownership of things, whether by corporation or socialist state, when confused with each other leads to the dislocation of person from responsible stewardship, whether in relation to corporation or social state, or indeed to actual private ownership itself. To establish tenable ground for a distinction between effective and ineffective ownership requires an inclusive metaphysics.

Tate's *real property*, insofar as it is in the control of the owner, is to be seen as an extension of person when the point is considered metaphysically. This is a recognition succinctly spoken to in the traditional shibboleth that a man's house is his castle. His property, in other words, is a *keep* of persons constituting a family. It is in relation to this implied metaphysical dimension of effective ownership that our laws of self-defense have traditionally extended to include a defense of that self's property.

XI. Ownership vs. Stewardship: Signposts at the Parting of Ways

This sense of a relationship of person to property is still very much extant in the South. The increasing legal civil assaults of the intruder upon victim, following his physical assault of personal property, makes a victim of an owner in both criminal and civil law. The burglar or thief or robber, who may have met comeuppance from the owner, is increasingly more protected than the actual owner. It is a shifting of the concept of property as personal that is baffling to one who accepts the tradition. The difficulty is that such a traditionalist is not prepared by metaphysical thought to defend himself against the growing dislocations in civil order. Was the burglar more than half way in the window when you shot him? If not, the burglar may have grounds for a suit against you for bodily harm. The sense of frustrated rage at such a proposition illustrates our general failure to establish a philosophical grounding of civil order. Of course, responsibility for actions in relation to ownership are at issue, and the traditional understanding is that one has a responsibility to defend his property but for reasons larger than mere possessiveness. The traditional defense of property is not merely understood as a right in relation to the value of the violated property but more centrally in relation to a violation of person, a violation of the office of responsibility of the owner to that which is his "property." The testimony of victims of burglary is heavy with their sense of having been personally violated, a reaction often puzzling to the victims themselves in our deracinated age.

Tate sensed that such responsibility was central to his concern, but he did not center upon that responsibility in its metaphysical dimension. Late in his "Notes" he said that "Responsibility is a function of control, and is necessary to effective ownership," and he added that a "responsibility of property" is an "attribute of property no less important than legal title itself." But put this way, his point is slightly askew. For responsibility is not merely a function of control; it is ultimately the justification of control, so that a failure to center that responsibility in *stewardship* leads to such villains in our lore as the miser and the wastrel. Responsibility is not "an attribute of property. It is rather an attribute of spiritual character, the spiritual aspect designated by the very term stewardship." To have clarified the point would have aligned Tate's central concern in respect to a tenable metaphysics of ownership.

The center of Tate's attack is on the joint-stock concept of property. The owner in relation to his fictions of material value—stocks, bonds, paper money—is reduced from personhood by the legalities founded in those fictions. Thus the owner as person will himself become an abstraction in relation to fictional property. Stock, in its actuality, is an abstraction out of an actual, real property, a portion of existential reality, as *owner* is an abstraction out of *person*. Stock stands surrogate to actual things but functions independent of those things and thereby complicates the responsibilities of human actions of stewardship toward actual materially existing things. Owner, a legal fiction, stands surrogate for person, a shield from responsibilities of stewardship. Thus as an abstraction, created by an abstractionist agent, the corporation supplants the actual person as owner. It is a fictional person, as Chief Justice Marshall declared it to be in that famous decision which Tate cited, the Dartmouth College Case of 1819.

The corporation, said Marshall in his decision, is "an artificial being, invisible, intangible, and existing only in contemplation of law. Being the mere creature of law, it possesses only those properties which the charter of its creation confers upon it, either expressly, or as incidental to its existence. Among the most important are immortality, and, if the expression may be allowed, individuality; properties by which a perpetual succession of many persons are considered as the same, and may act as a single individual." It is thus that, by a positing of words, this fictional person, who is legally declared both immortal and individual by virtue of a Nominalistic summary of its pseudo-essence, is defined by its charter. That is, it is thus fictionally "embodied." The corporation thereby becomes a stalking horse of aggression against material existence when abused by its manipulators, who are themselves actual and not fictional "individuals." Because of the incorporated fiction, it becomes possible that these individuals may set aside responsibilities of stewardship, although

XI. Ownership vs. Stewardship: Signposts at the Parting of Ways

one may not say that all persons thus related to corporations have ignored or do ignore personal responsibility. That is, some persons, though cloaked in the immortal garb of a corporation, still manage to exercise responsible governance of the actual property fallen to the legal, state sanctioned, control of that abstract "person," the corporation. But the legalized fiction of incorporation nevertheless establishes a legal ground for excluding the responsibilities of stewardship, though in our current panic over the environment, we increasingly attempt to legislate stewardship.

The corporation has become accepted under the authority of established law as a legal fiction, an immortal nonsubstantial body whose existence is decreed by words through the will of intellects— those certifying persons (judges) operating in the name of another abstraction, the state. In concert, these establish the laws of the mortal communities of men. It is thus we are led to accept a fiction as a reality. This pseudo-essence carries a pseudo-lifeblood stock whose function is to register abstractly and relatively its pseudo-life. Thus the public display of the "stock market" in which corporations are measured as if they were patients in hospital. They are hovered over by a variety of pseudo-doctor specialists who give the anxious public a running account of their growing strength or sad decline. And indeed, Justice Marshall was wrong in asserting that the corporation is immortal. Many have passed as if in the way of all flesh, to speak fictionally. Once existing fictions, they are now evaporated almost absolutely, though they may have left traces in our economic histories.

Such is the pseudo-metaphysical nature with which the putative owner, the possessor of stock in a corporation, must relate himself as owner. As Tate says, what such an owner quickly discovers is that he has no effective control of the *actual* property which is manipulated for good or ill by the mortal wearers of the immortal corporate robes, the operators and managers of corporate interests. Those operators are putively agents on behalf of stock owners. They are so, however, in relation to the actual property stamped by corporate logo.

We have come to the point of Tate's concern, in relation to what we have argued as the responsibility of a stewardship of the world's body as exercised variously by putative and actual owners of portions of that body. We must remember that this fictional person, the corporation, exercises actual control over actual, real things. To take Tate's example, the name United States Steel Corporation signifies, despite its abstract character, a complex of actual things—buildings, machines, iron ore, mines, and so on and on. It is at this juncture of fictional existence, the corporation, with reality—with actually existing things, its power over actual property—that difficulty arises out of the fictional "nature" of the corporation. And it is a concern which can be adequately addressed only metaphysically, if one is to discover why one sort of property, namely stock, by its very nature as an abstraction of nature, effectively deposes its putative owner from the real property as manipulated in his name by the corporation. We understand, here, that—as Tate also recognized—what is said of the *corporation* applies equally to the *socialist* state. They are bloodless brothers, though possessing a fictionalized blood.

At this juncture, then, Tate locates that small "clique" of directors who wield effective or ineffective control of that real property which constitutes something like United States Steel Corporation. They are excused their responsibility of actual ownership, unless they choose to embrace that responsibility, because they are subject not to nature nor to the God of nature but only to that abstract person, the corporation as defined by the state. The "director" of a corporation, in whose charge are the actual laborers with the actual real property, hardly stands in relation to his conglomerate of stockholders, as the steward of old stood in relation to the lord of the manor. Indeed, the intellectually devised legal climate justifies such a director in that perverse address to the world's body which Eric Voegelin describes as modern gnosticism. Such a gnostic is concerned with an absolute control over being itself. One might compare for distinction the relation of a director of an international corporation to the relation of the local mom-pop store to mom or pop. But we must insist that the issue here is not efficiency or productivity or size or any of the virtues proper

XI. Ownership vs. Stewardship: Signposts at the Parting of Ways

to the ordering of any business in the public interest. We are concerned rather for the dangers inherent in the legal conditions governing the presence or absence of a sense of stewardship. They are dangers whose consequences have been effected by legalized fictions, devastatingly illustrated in our century by the corporation on the one hand and the socialist state on the other.

Considered in another perspective, the loyalty of those engaged on behalf of the putative owners is hardly to those owners as persons, whether we mean the loyalty of the director or regional manager or laborer to the actual stockholder. That loyalty, a name echoing (if but remotely) the concept of responsibility, is nevertheless recognized as required in some degree. There is a lingering, residual sense of responsibility of person to person in respect to actual property. At the most pragmatic level of concern, loyalty is required in relation to an efficiency of operation, of process, whereby the fictional person receives a good or bad health report on the stock exchange in relation to its art of making things of one sort or another. And the larger the corporation—not in respect to its putative or fictional, but to the actual property under its control—the greater the recognition of the importance of "loyalty" to that fiction. John Crowe Ransom was quite right that a person "cannot contemplate nor explore, respect nor love, a mere turnover, such as an assemblage of natural resources," a pile of money, a volume of produce, a market, a credit system, save if he is that rarity among persons, the distorted miser, some Ebenezer Scrooge. Hence in the dilemma those attempts, and often at considerable expense through public relations programs internally and externally focused, to substantiate the corporation through building a sense of loyalty to the "company." The company becomes a fictional object, symbolized by its logo, upon which a worker is encouraged to focus his innate desire as a person: the desire to assume responsibility as steward of existential reality. It is in the name of the company, then, that the worker *makes*, and not under the larger auspices of the Cause of all making.

The concern of corporate leadership for a unity whereby common labor is focused upon the things being made is a valid concern, though excesses in that concern occur and are sometimes caricatured in satiric comedy about company loyalty. But what corporate leadership is very likely to ignore, or not even recognize, is that this necessity to the discrete person in his devotion to making is founded in his innate nature. No company as such is its cause. It is a desire out of an intuitive recognition of the responsibility of stewardship in making, and it is a responsibility to be exercised through art. That is, the exercise is of the essential nature of man himself as maker. That we here speak of *industrial* art primarily, of the process of *manufacture*—a "making by hands"—does not lessen but rather intensifies the point.

Indeed, the destructive nature of industrialism due to its being divorced from responsible stewardship has fragmented the desired "loyalty" within the general community of workers to the point that a recovery has become crucial to corporate interest. What is true of corporate interest is true as well of political interest, and out of the same hungers intrinsic to human nature. At a time when the state as an abstraction, manipulated by ineffective and corrupt politicians in a betrayal of those hungers, the transgressions of stewardship have reduced the voting public to cynicism. The problem is susceptible to a satisfactory solution only when the corporate mentality (or its kindred, the political mentality) recovers and accepts the underlying principles legitimizing its pragmatic concern for productivity or for good government. Loyalty as understood by the popular mind clearly affects productivity, but only out of the *essential* nature of man himself as maker. (I have expanded this concept at length in *Making: The Proper Habit of Our Being*.)

There is a further concession to the necessity of loyalty, often exploited in recent corporate history: the entitlement of managers to stock in the company. And there is an additional development that has become somewhat more popular since World War II: the enfranchisement of the laborers themselves in the abstract corporation by stock ownership—a move that has often proved immediate in its effects upon the pragmatic efficiency of some companies or corpora-

XI. Ownership vs. Stewardship: Signposts at the Parting of Ways

tions. It tends to effectiveness because it helps recover ownership substantively to the material aspect of a corporation. The laborer becomes interested as part owner of what he is making with his hands. At least every four years a similar attempt is made in the political sphere, with the excited news to the general populace of its new enfranchisement in the state by virtue of the vote. That we are less successful here is indicated in the cynical position taken by the voting public toward office holders here at the funeral of the century.

A final observation in regard to Tate's concern for our loss of real ownership through fictional manipulations of the realities of nature itself: at our own moment, more than fifty years after his essay, there is a growing emphasis toward reconciling actual persons to the fictional person, both to the state and to the corporation. The emphasis begins to be centered in a newly recovered concern for stewardship, always latent in the essential nature of the person as person, as I have insisted. In this era, stewardship as a corporate responsibility is very much an issue on the political and social stages. Good husbandry of the things accumulated in the name of a corporation is advertised as the corporation's significant virtue, in elaborate and sometimes stunningly Edenesque ads on the evening television. At the moment at least the thematic emphasis of corporate advertising, especially by the largest corporations, turns on its environmental piety. If trees are down, more trees are planted "by good corporate management." Wildlife, water, soil are to be balanced against harvest.

Even should one be so cynical as to allow that this new address to stewardship by the corporate mentality has been forced by necessity, like the forced conversion of pagans, it is still a welcomed development, to be accepted and supported by good reason. It is to be welcomed because it is a change, however slight, toward recovery of a metaphysics of stewardship. We shall have to come to terms with the necessity, but at a level of intellectual concern deeper than the *ad hoc* arguments of the management's concern for worker morale, or in a wider perspective the arguments of environmental science which lacks metaphysical dimension. Stewardship, we must rediscover, requires the arts of husbanding essences, whether such husbandry be applied to farms or forests or factories. Tate might have argued very much in this train of thought by the 1950s, at which time he had become widely parted philosophically from his old teacher and fellow poet, Ransom. Tate did not abandon his Agrarian concerns. Rather, he attempted to put them in a larger perspective.

By the 1950s Ransom's philosophy clearly rested in the principle of scientific specialization as adapted to the making of order in words, as we have seen. It is a philosophy which at its inception in 18th century rationalism turned to technological addresses to material existence, to what Ransom called in his famous metaphorical phrase the "world's body." But that address of technological specialization is incompatible to the spiritual requirement of stewardship which is the implicit ground of the Agrarians' argument. That the Agrarians submitted so variously to that requirement was inevitable because they had not fully developed the philosophical ground of the requirement. At that point of our history, the 1930s, the new industrial spirit, like its companion the new political spirit, had rather thoroughly established abstraction as the god of specialization in justification of Utopian pursuits. The one Utopian idea is the fictional corporation, the other the fictional state as ultimate mother of mankind. Both are at once founded *in* and *by* their fruits, effects shallowly understood but accepted as justifications of specialized science. That is, specialized science as the limited knowing of the mystery of nature becomes both a self-justifying principle and the instrument to the reordering of nature, including human nature. Ransom's specialized science of art, as was uncomfortably apparent to Tate, was out of the same thought as the specialized science of corporate industry and of the modern state.

There is reason for some hope, we have suggested. The "industrial complex" is slowly recovering itself. It may continue to do so, but only insofar as it recovers, through its actual, mortal directors, a metaphysical perspective. The point must be insisted upon again and again. What is necessary is that persons in positions of responsibility, whether directors or laborers or owners of stock, accept the moral responsibility of their concrete actions upon the actual things of nature, ranging from material things to persons—from corn or cotton, or trees and streams, or machines and the things made by machines by the local laborer. To be consumed by a thankful community of persons deployed in their several offices of stewardship, recovered as members of a communal body of persons: a recovered community.

The necessary art of a husbandry of existential reality, under the rubric of responsible stewardship, lies in a prudential virtue which can be resident only in the husbanding person. This has been a difficult lesson to learn, and one confused by alarms and excesses from all quarters of the intellectual community. It is a lesson still dim and uncertain to our understanding, but one which can be focused in relation to responsible actions of both making and using, as I am sure Tate would say to us in the 21st century. That focus will be effective only through a realistic metaphysics, a recovery of intellect to reality out of its Cartesian-Kantian wanderings over the recent centuries through more or less desert landscapes. Such high sentences said, let us turn more directly and closely to Allen Tate as a pilgrim slowly coming to such recognitions about man's place in the world and his consequent responsibilities to the world. His was not an abandonment of his early Agrarianism, we have said, but an enlargement of and substantiation of its principles through his concerns for a Thomistic realism. This is to say once more that the metaphysical orientation necessary to the recovery of viable community requires the vision of history's relation to nature as under the auspices of the transcendent Cause of complex reality, of that whole of creation.

XII

The "Cranky" Distinction Between Poetry and Religion

Richard Weaver, who supported the Southern Agrarian concern with influential essays (as for instance his very effective *Ideas Have Consequences*), echoed Tate's argument made in "Remarks on the Southern Religion," Tate's contribution to *I'll Take My Stand*. In his own address to "The Older Religiousness of the South" (*Sewanee Review*, 1943), Weaver remarked that "The South did not want a reasoned belief, but a satisfying dogma." There is sufficient justification to such a summary statement to give us pause. "Among all the classes in the South," Weaver added, "an opinion obtained that religion should be a sentiment." The Southerner's desire was for a comfortable rest in nature, untroubled by intellectual necessities, and it was perhaps desirable for a reason Weaver put thus: "Man cannot live under a settled dispensation if the postulates of his existence must be continually revised in accordance with knowledge furnished by a nature filled with contingencies."

Certainly from the mid–1800s, those contingencies began to be intrusive upon this Southern inclination to rest intellect in the seeming constancy of nature, as science more and more confidently probed nature. The upheavals of the industrial revolution as increasingly supported by Darwinian evolution was a confluence of ideas in which new doctrines about nature's contingencies pressed more and more upon intellectual complacency. Tate lamented that complacency was too typically Southern, this rest in religion as a mere sentiment which

XII. The "Cranky" Distinction Between Poetry and Religion

left the Southerner exposed to modernist assaults. But Tate was aware of the problem earlier than in his essay in *I'll Take My Stand*. "What shall we say" to this intrusion, Tate had asked in his most famous poem, "Ode to the Confederate Dead." "What shall we say who have knowledge/ Carried to the heart."

Tate would later remind us in a note to his poem that he had in mind in his phrase "knowledge carried to the heart" Pascal's "war between heart and head." And that is the "war" he concentrated upon in his first Agrarian essay, developing his concern in his metaphor of the half-horse, the once unified horse now divided against itself by 1930. As for Pascal's metaphor of heart and head, we know that Pascal was aware of that Western intellectual tradition, especially prevalent in our poetry, whereby the intuitive intellect is associated with the heart, the rational intellect with the head. The most arresting—and extended—use of the Thomistic principle of intellect as unified, in which the rational is an extension of the intuitive, is the metaphor dramatized in Dante's *Divine Comedy*. Virgil, mentor to the pilgrim Dante's rational faculty, leads Dante through Hell and up Purgatory Mountain. On that journey the pilgrim Dante is strengthened toward a recovery of the validity of his intuitive faculty. Through his reassociation of those faculties under the guidance of Beatrice, this pilgrim poet is prepared for the concluding beatific vision. Nearer our own day, the "dissociation of sensibility," the separation of, and diverse specializations of, heart and head, is made famous in literary criticism by T. S. Eliot. It is reflected in the significantly divided aspect of 18th century Rationalism as countered by 19th century Romanticism, the reductions and separation implicit in Cartesianism. Out of the subsequent confusions concerning our intellectual faculties, there arises that considerable concern for epistemology in the 19th and 20th centuries, but not a concern limited to the poet. For, as Gilson reminded us, the concern leads to an obsession in modern philosophy with epistemology as the principal problem to rational thought.

Certainly poets like Tate and Eliot turned back to Dante, in whom they found exhibited a persuasive association of heart and head. And certainly Pascal was one of the mediators of their turning, as both acknowledged. In *Pensées*, for instance, Pascal insisted: "We know the truth not only by reason but more so by the heart. It is in this latter way that we know first principles, and it is vain that reason, which plays no part in this, tries to combat them." It could but be encouraging to Eliot in the early 1920s and to Tate by 1930 that Pascal found his own way out of his initial adamant rejection of Christianity. Pascal, a sophisticated young intellectual devoted to skepticism, found that deportment insufficient. Skepticism unsettles intellectual certainty. Especially it disturbs reason's certainty that intellect is autonomous.

If the intellect's confidence in its own power of understanding is once called in question, it becomes possible that the arrested intellect may, with fear and trembling, move beyond its arrest. Out of skepticism grows faith—by grace. Or so Pascal would argue. We might observe in this relation of skepticism to spiritual recovery that the skepticism which Pascal observes in himself cannot find rest in Stoicism as classically formulated. That was to be a discovery traumatically significant to Eliot, who turned his own distressing uncertainty in an effective opening of his closed intellect toward the mystery of existence, including the mystery of himself as person. He turned to the mystery of being itself out of his spiritual crisis in 1920–22. Such was the spiritual crisis whose issue is *The Waste Land*.

It hardly needs adding, surely, that this movement out of skepticism requires the full uses of the reason in relation to the mystery whereby intellect finds itself possessed of a knowledge of first principles before it discovers the uses of its rational faculty. The rational faculty is necessary to confirm the experience of first principles known before any rationalization of them. Thus reason fulfills intuitive knowledge, intuitive knowledge being the initiating effect through grace of action in finite intellect. Who would deny that both Tate and Eliot are among our most sophisticated intellectual poets? But their reasoned support of their position, once they come to themselves in our dark modernist woods, is in support of their intuitive knowledge.

XII. The "Cranky" Distinction Between Poetry and Religion

They move out of the skepticism which was *de rigueur* to the sophisticated intellectual in the first two decades of this century, the intellectual community these poets were committed to.

The disturbing circumstance of the Southern temperament as characterized by Richard Weaver, as Tate recognized in 1930, is that its heart's knowledge is severely called in question. It is called in question by an alien rationalism at a point in human history when that Southern temperament has long since lost the grounding of its sentiment by rational intellect in any metaphysical vision. That is the handicap which Richard Weaver explored, following Tate. What this division of intellect means is that the settled confidence of the Southern temperament is eroded. The same proves true, of course, of viable communities far removed from the South. As the Agrarian symposiasts say in their preface, "Proper living is a matter of intelligence and the will, does not depend on the local climate or geography, and is capable of a definition which is general and not Southern at all." In this respect, the Southern context out of which the Agrarians address the question of a religious deportment in their local climate and geography, in pursuit of a proper living, is an accident of history in respect to the essential nature of such a proper living. That is why Stark Young in his contribution insists that the Agrarians defend "certain qualities not because they belong to the South, but because the South belongs to them."

Religion as a sentiment, residual to intellect but insufficiently supported by knowledge justified by reason, cannot give intellect the confidence needed to hold and clarify its actions in nature as proportionately ordered by a nature existing under the overarching and permeating keep of nature's God. What other effect than chaotic intellectual alarm at the intrusion of alien suppositions could result? The Agrarian statement of "Principles" speaks to the concern. "Religion is our submission to the general intention of a nature that is fairly inscrutable; it is the sense of our role as creatures within it." But under the impetus of the alien God spawned by that autonomous intellect which thereby assumes itself transcendent of nature, made manifest in industrialism, we "receive the illusion of having power over nature, and lose the sense of nature as something mysterious and contingent." Then follow the telling words, ironic in the light of our exploration of Ransom's divergence from this position since he is the principal author of this statement of principles: "The God of nature under these conditions is merely an amiable expression, a superfluity, and the philosophical understanding ordinarily carried in the religious experience is not there for us to have."

By the late 1930s, rather certainly Ransom's own view of "God" is of an "amiable expression," a superfluity when philosophically addressed. But it is that "philosophical understanding" that Tate and Davidson (and others of the Agrarians) are concerned to recover to the argument, against the inclination of the modernist's reduction of the necessity to the soul to worship the God of all things. After 1918, the lines are drawn around the chaotic world, making it a stage for intellect's actions. The stage was set for that next devastating war, World War II, as a consequence of ideas in conflict which had reached no resolution and so were ideas of destructive consequence. The concern for recovering philosophical understanding of man's relation to nature and to nature's God led the Agrarians to take a stand, with some help from various allies—the Neo-Thomists, the Distributists, the Humanists at Harvard. In differing ways, all these opposed the increasingly triumphant power of secular gnosticism which operates on the principle that finite intellect is the only transcendent. That aberrant position seems justified by its uses of nature and society. That is, it accumulated a formidable power. At the level of spectacle, and to the considerable confusion of those who attempted to oppose modern gnosticism's spectacular effects, the events on the closed world stage served only to confuse the issue. For different species of gnostic power were discovered in conflict with each other in greater and greater acts of destruction of the stage itself. A symptom to the point: recall the initial alliance of Hitler and Stalin, followed by the subsequent alliance of Stalin and the "democratic" powers of the West, followed by that forty-year war made popular as the "Cold War."

XII. The "Cranky" Distinction Between Poetry and Religion

To the Agrarian mind, observing the disintegration of the Western intellectual community, it could but appear evident that our world was bent on intensifying an old chaos which Matthew Arnold in a melancholy moment and on the edge of despair described in a once famous poem. Here on this "darkling plain/Swept with confused alarms of struggle and flight," we are engulfed by "ignorant armies" that "clash by night," he says. Ransom might well have been led to take metaphorical direction out of Arnold, turning to literary formalism in his own specialization of intellectual reason in service to his own word, given such dark vision of the historical moment. "Ah, love," Arnold had lamented, "let us be true to one another!" That is our last best hope, because the world about us is in all its seeming beauty but an illusion, one in which there is "neither joy, nor love, nor light,/Nor certitude, nor peace, nor help for pain." In that act of attention to the literary text as one's "True Penelope" as Ezra Pound characterizes his retreat, a poet may withdraw from the darkling plain. Only thus does there seem some solace to intellect. But neither Tate nor Davidson could find solace in such a love affair of intellect with the literary text. They were drawn into the continuing battle, however much they might appear, from a position of ironic detachment, to be rather like Ransom's Captain Carpenter. They, like Captain Carpenter, though repeatedly unhorsed and increasingly maimed, always once more "sallied from the gate in hell's despite" to seek out their enemies, those enemies of the abiding truth of things carried to the heart.

The Agrarian position, as announced by its "Statement of Principles," resists the reduction of man until he must be concluded but a part of nature at his greatest. But it finds itself doing so from a position insufficiently grounded in "philosophical understanding." As poets, some of these Agrarians were aware that, since the 18th century, there had occurred progressively the dissociation of sensibility, the separation of heart and head, of the intuitive from the rational intellect, which Eliot had characterized in his famous essay "The Metaphysical Poets" (1921). Such, said Eliot, is the loss of "a fidelity to [both] thought and feeling." That was an argument Eliot made just as the Fugitives became active as lyric poets. The separation of thought and feeling had been long underway, much longer than the rupture at the time of Dryden and Milton, where Eliot located the dissociation. But by 1930 it was no longer possible to deny its effects in the social, economic, and political spheres, concerns more deconstructively pervasive of community than the limited concerns of the poet for his art—his poem taken as his ultimate Beatrice.

To put the matter bluntly, there had been for some centuries a civil war which proved even more destructive in its 20th century manifestation than the spectacular war on the American continent in the 1860s. It is this intellectual war, as separate from the spectacle of political division and wartime slaughter, whether in the 19th or 20th centuries, that the Agrarians were attempting to affect. They did so initially in relation to history, a concept they did not fully expound upon in its philosophical implications. Nevertheless, we find them individually pursuing a philosophical understanding in biographies of fellow Southerners. But, given the seemingly topical nature of their elected figures, the significant concern in their attempt at recovering the philosophical ground long abandoned was easily overlooked, and sometimes even deliberately misrepresented as a concern for provincialism.

Tate wrote his biography of Stonewall Jackson, in Paris. At home, Lytle wrote his *Bedford Forrest and his Critter Company*. John Donald Wade, in Georgia, wrote his *John Wesley*, exploring that continuing influence on Southern religion. Warren turned to an antagonist reviled by the South, John Brown. There was as well another species of exploration of the Southern mind, as variously pursued as in Ransom's *The World's Body* and Davidson's *Attack on Leviathan*. For in the pursuit of history as consequential to continuing ideas, perhaps there lay the possibility of a recovery of knowledge viable to the intellectual community, now rapidly dissolving through conflicting ideologies. Nevertheless, the spectacle of history addressed, by its concentration on the 1860s as the seeming center, made the Agrarians'

XII. The "Cranky" Distinction Between Poetry and Religion

antagonists themselves limit the concern to the local, the topical. These Southerners were embittered by Appomattox. They wanted merely to "turn back the clock" to refight that local war. We have not, after more than fifty years, succeeded in freeing the argument of provincial concerns. And the distorting provincialism, alas, is practiced on both sides. One must have a sympathy with Ransom's growing weariness over "patriotism" as a banner disputed by ignorant armies, clashing under a provincial darkness.

Of this various knowledge, that of heart and that of head, Weaver in his essay remarked that "though probably no people were more ignorant of the *Summa Theologica* than the inarticulate and little-read Southern population, this Thomistic dualism lies implicit in their opposition to scientific monism." Indeed, this is "the most persistent of the South's medieval heritages." We observe in passing that Weaver's is a remarkably apt suggestion about the "Southern" weakness, though it is not couched with a sufficient precision of terms, as our opening chapters will have shown. For we are not dealing with a "Thomistic dualism." St. Thomas is most emphatic in his opposition to the Averroist heresy of intellect as dual, and his treatise *On the Unity of the Intellect Against the Averroists* makes that point quite clear. Intellect to the singular person is unified, but in its operations within the singular intellect it may be seen analytically (by rational intellect as we say) as both intuitive and as rational. However, the rational, says St. Thomas, aware of the dangers of dualism if he is misunderstood, is an "extension" of the intuitive nature, not a separate nature to intellect. [12]

That had been the point of Tate's own departure in his essay in *I'll Take My Stand*. But having to "think for oneself" as he had to do for his essay was "a responsibility intolerable to the religious mind." Consequently, he began in "a spirit of irreligion" so he could think for himself. The South in its intellectual position, depending on sentiment and not intellect in respect to religion, afforded him little ground as a "natural" Southerner in which he could stand against the encroaching enemy, who was made manifest by rationalist science through science's principal weapon, the encroaching industrialism managed by Big Business. He knew that this invading enemy had as its principle of operation an address to complex reality which is deadly to spirit: "abstraction is the death of religion." What is required, as the Southern temperament has been slow to recognize, is a recovery of reason to the support of intuitive knowledge. That is the necessary reassociation of intellectual faculties which Tate would gradually come to champion, partly through his reading of Eliot, but largely under the tutelage of Jacques Maritain, his World War II friend. In that progress, he would come to see that reason is not necessarily the "spirit of irreligion," as he earlier proposed.

That he comes to such an understanding is reflected in a letter he wrote Donald Davidson after World War II, after sharply castigating Ransom's treatment of Eliot's *Complete Poems* in a recent *New Republic* essay. Ransom's essay makes "a completely cranky and untenable point which distinguishes poetry from religion. Religion and the 'mysteries' are for people who have a sense of sin. Poetry is 'appearances' presumably for people who delight in the sensible world without sin." We have argued that Tate's evaluation is quite accurate as to Ransom's position, and it is a position not only incipient in Ransom from the beginning, but more and more explicitly established by Ransom in the decade of the 1930s. Again, it was not a position arrived at late in life.

What troubled Tate most about Ransom's late review were the allusions to the old Agrarian days. Ransom suggested, he said, that "we never got much further than Nostalgia because no historical faith came into consideration." On reflection about that point, Tate added, "I think there's a great deal in that. We were trying to find a religion in the secular, the historical experience as such, particularly in the Old South. I would now go further than John and say we were idolaters. But it is better to be an idolater than to worship nothing." Or, as his scathing evaluation of Ransom's criticism of Eliot suggested, better to worship history than art, since by the idolatry of history one is at least forced back toward an encounter with one's fellows on the

XII. The "Cranky" Distinction Between Poetry and Religion

plains of history, while art allows a withdrawal to Parnassian heights in a separation from both heaven and earth, a withdrawal that the always fiery Tate would see as cowardice. ("John rejects religion and takes poetry. I wonder whether he felt that he was without sin.") What Tate, in his letter of 1952, did not seem to remember was that his present concern about history was the nagging concern in his own essay about religion in the South, way back in 1930, though he was not so bold then as to force the issue of possible idolatry. But he was already acutely aware at that early time of the dangers to intellect out of its "dissociated sensibilities." Eliot's earlier and somewhat shallow concern became limited to literary concerns. Eliot then, like Ransom later, had chosen poetry over religion and rational intellect over intuitive intellect. The early Eliot as hero to Tate left him disquieted, but with some difficulty in thinking through the course of his intellectual discomfort.

As for Tate's position in that early essay, he began with a demurrer to the volume's title, *I'll Take My Stand*. "It emphasizes the fact of exclusiveness rather than its benefits; it points to a particular house but omits to say that it was the home of a spirit that may also have lived elsewhere and that this mansion, in short, was incidentally made with hands." In short, Tate's fear was that the Agrarian position as defended in the symposium may be entrapped in history, and in a history not sufficiently open to the larger flow of spirit Westward as guided by orthodox theology. Such a history is limited. He had already rejected it in his famous words, contemporary to Eliot's "Ash-Wednesday" and Davidson's *Tall Men*, poems both of which show a community of understanding among these three poets, a community closer than Davidson himself could at that moment see. Davidson's *Tall Men*, in fact, is an attack on *The Waste Land*, though on grounds quite other than Ransom's early attack on that poem.[13]

The most celebrated passage from Tate's "Ode to the Confederate Dead" serves beautifully as a summary of his own spiritual disquiet, but one must be aware of the quality of the irony in it as distinguished from Ransom's irony: it is sardonic, the words turned back upon the speaker who is suspended between a past, tradition as affected by orthodoxy, and present, modernism in its ruthless reductions of the human spirit:

> What shall we say who have knowledge
> Carried to the heart? Shall we take the act
> To the grave? Shall we, more hopeful, set up the grave
> In the house? The ravenous grave? [14]

What Tate knew intuitively in these words, but what he would have to struggle to recover to rational explication, is the necessity of a viable metaphysical vision whereby history and nature are accommodated beyond those separations of history from nature which have made possible the violations of the world's body by both the modernist spirit and the more shallow traditionalist, made so by a reductionist faith in history. (The modernist and the shallow traditionalist in this perspective are both sons of Hegel.) That has proved a spirit not easily exorcised by any struggling intellect's attempt to recover the faint path in our dark woods, especially the dark woods of disoriented intellect. The sort of rationalization of modernism that becomes more and more explicit in Ransom cannot be effectively countered by the sort of intuitive knowledge in the heart that allows as its only defense of truth the setting up of the grave—"history"—in the house.

Davidson, incidentally, addressed this same problem in his "On a Replica of the Parthenon," a poem in which he sees with scathing irony this spirit of modernism in its commercial manifestation, its appropriation of a shallow traditionalism. The Nashville business leaders set up in the city the "grave" of Classical Greece in the interest of profit, their elaborate reproduction of the Greek Parthenon. Davidson's concluding lines are admonitory about this false temple summoning commerce and placating conscience. It is not wisdom here honored, but evidence of a "blind motion" spawned in conscience as a "dim last/regret of men who slew their past" and now raise up "this bribe against their fate." In his essay on Southern religion, then, Tate understood the danger of history divorced from

XII. The "Cranky" Distinction Between Poetry and Religion

nature by abstractionism, an intellectually blind motion whatever bribes it may raise against fate. To the modern mind, history is only "an idea, an abstraction, a concept," he said. To set up history in this aspect is to set up the grave in the house. As put in the figure he extended in his essay, history so taken is "the religion of the half-horse," the religion ultimately of "how things work." It is but half the horse, since separated from the complexity of creation by an irrationality assumed to be rationality, namely a belief "in omnipotent human rationality."

What has been lost, as Tate argued, is the wisdom of the medieval doctors. For the medieval Church, by "making Reason, Science, or Nature, an instrument of defense for the protection of the other than reasonable [the intuitively known], the other than natural ... performed a tremendous feat of spiritual unity, and the one kind of unity that the Western mind is capable of." Having lost that wisdom of reason in support of intuitive intellect, the South is incapable of articulating the virtue of knowledge carried to the heart intuitively, a viable knowledge differing from the lesser knowledge achieved through science itself. It is a failure out of a mistake: "Simply because it tried to encompass its destiny within the terms of Protestantism, in origin, a non-agrarian and trading religion," it becomes seduced internally at last by "secular ambition."[15]

One might say, as Tate didn't quite say, that so disarmed, Southern leadership (especially that of the South's political leaders) had too thoroughly embraced John Locke. For who better than Locke is suited to the abstract, modern mind? Who more suspicious of the intuitive? That this is so requires only our remembering on the one hand Locke's advice to parents to beat poetry out of the young with a stick early in their lives and the anomalous position of Lockean rationality as a substitute for metaphysical vision. To such a rationalist, in Tate's words, there is "not much difference between a centaur ... and Christ ... because both are mythical figments answerable to the same 'laws.'" One might suggest that such Lockean pragmatism crossed with Cartesian idealism leads to Kantian rationalism such as Ransom embraced, and we may notice the consequence in his poetry, as we have noticed it in his *Kenyon Review* phase, where he was prepared in his pluralism to accept Christ as an amiable expression, a term comforting to the unsophisticated.

Ransom's irony carefully shielded him from a commitment, not only to Christ or a centaur, but to any sentiment drawing intellect too dangerously into the immediate, proximate world, that world which was Tate's and Davidson's concern. On the point, compare the uses of irony in "Captain Carpenter" on the one hand and "Bells for John Whiteside's Daughter" on the other. Surely I need not say that the point here is separate from a concern for virtues of those poems as art. We are rather concerned, as we have been all along, with the philosophical grounds out of which Ransom's art proceeds, and with whether it is suited to that community of mankind in history that was Tate's and Davidson's principal concern. In praise of art, but as limited in its possibilities, then, the following, lest I be misunderstood:

Art is effective insofar as its formal perfections address the desire for an accommodation of intellect to the mystery of existence itself. Its desirable tensions, however well balanced by the virtues of art, must reflect an inadequacy of art in and of itself to make the desired reconciliation of intellect to reality. That is why one has as an effect in art—the comic, the pathetic, the tragic—those effects out of the insufficiency of man as maker to fully reconcile himself to creation. When Aristotle speaks of catharsis, when Milton speaks of that state of mind and spirit in which one knows "all passion spent," they are speaking of art's limited uses in moving the soul toward a reconciliation beyond its own finite powers to accomplish. It moves a way toward reconciliation, but it cannot move all the way, the final transit possible only through grace.

One moves beyond art's inadequacies, though it would be churlish to reject art's service in helping move one toward reconciliation. What is necessary is that intellect not make the mistake of supposing art itself the origin of the grace needed to satisfy our intellectual hope

XII. The "Cranky" Distinction Between Poetry and Religion

for a rest in truth. Art is a good, but a lesser good, in the economy of the soul. That is a lesson Tate learned, not without considerable agonies of soul, in turning to Thomistic metaphysics. It is a lesson, I suspect, which Donald Davidson knew rather well intuitively. It is a lesson John Crowe Ransom rather resolutely set aside, choosing at last to believe in the oblivion of intellect as man's final end. He had long since abandoned the illusion of *God*, that "amiable expression" conceded by the latest theologians to the hoi polloi to comfort them in their bereavement over the loss of a loved one.

Afterword

Since the publication of *I'll Take My Stand* in 1930, there have been a number of distinguished intellectuals firmly committed to realism over idealism, many of them having helped restore our "philosophical understanding" of the ordinate relation of intellect to nature and to nature's God. One thinks of such formidable minds as C. S. Lewis, Tolkien, Maritain, Gilson, Marcel, Voegelin, and Niemeyer. The list can be easily extended. It needs to be observed, however, that some among such an extended listing find themselves somewhat uneasy at the suggestion that the Agrarians are allies. An early expression of that uncertainty is Eliot's in *After Strange Gods*, his Page-Barbour Lectures at the University of Virginia published in 1933. The lectures were given in an environment in which Ransom had defended Agrarian concerns in formal debates. Eliot's opening statement begins with an expressed unhappiness with his own earlier position in "Tradition and the Individual Talent" (1921), and he at once engages the term *tradition*, citing the concern of the Agrarians in *I'll Take My Stand*. He is "much interested" in these recent writers whose topic is tradition, desiring to see "further statements by the same group of writers." At this same time, Tate had proposed a second volume of essays to Eugene F. Saxton at Harper & Brothers, a collection which would include an essay by Eliot himself on "The Pseudo-Religious Character of the Extreme Determinists' Ideas of Economics." The volume never developed, though Tate's concern led at last to *Who Owns America?* three years later. And so Eliot never joins with the Agrarians directly.

Afterword

Eliot wanted to see further statements by these emerging polemicists most probably because he, like Tate in his contribution to the Agrarian volume, was uncertain of the sense in which the Agrarians addressed themselves to the concept of tradition. He found his own address to tradition in his earlier essay specifically lacking in that it is too much limited. He could not in 1933 treat such a topic "as a purely literary one." Indeed, *After Strange Gods* is an enlargement of his earlier concern in which he attempted to define a difference between *tradition* and *orthodoxy*. It is only from the point of view of orthodoxy that he could then begin to understand the nature of the individual talent.

Polemical events in the late 1930s in relation to Agrarian arguments continue to cloud our response to their position even today. Especially this is true among poets and fiction writers who in notable ways are supportive of the basic propositions enunciated in *I'll Take My Stand*. One might explore this point, for instance, in Robert Lowell, Ransom's student at Kenyon and Tate's friend. The same disquiet one might find in Robert Fitzgerald, Flannery O'Connor's supportive friend. (It was in part through her acquaintance with the Fitzgeralds that she became for a time a close friend of Robert Lowell though increasingly uneasy about his wavering intellectual position.)

But for our concluding observation, it is sufficient to recall another of O'Connor's friends who is also another considerable Southern writer, Walker Percy. As late as 1980, Percy said of the Agrarians, "I never fitted in with those fellows," since "My South was always the New South. My first memories are of the country club, of people playing golf." Those "fellows" he understood here as having primarily celebrated "the traditional virtues of the South while denouncing the corrupt industrial North." It is as if Percy forgot how effectively he himself denounced that corrupt industrialism as the father of consumerism, while at the same time he gave his untenable characterization of the Fugitive-Agrarian concern. We should remember, for instance, that these "fellows ... who called themselves Fugitives" (Percy's words) are quite explicit about the Southern tradition Percy saddled them with. In their "Foreword" to the first issue of *The Fugitive* they say: "THE FUGITIVE flees from nothing faster than from the high-caste Brahmins of the Old South." Percy saw himself as a fugitive Southerner, fleeing both Old and New South. Among the observations to be noted in relation to Percy's distancing himself from such fellows as Tate was that Percy managed to come "home" even earlier than his fellow Southerner Tate. That is, he entered the Roman Church three years before Tate made that move.

Walker Percy was a Southerner who made his way, with great difficulty, back to Mother Church. His journey was parallel to Tate's. He was set back on his intellectual heels in a dark moment of his life by reading Kierkegaard and the *Summa Theologica*. It is of ironic interest, then, that he seemed always cautious to set a distance between himself and the Agrarians, in contrast to that friend whose work he so much admired, Flannery O'Connor. In an interview given just before his death (published in *Crisis*, September 1990), he had moved considerably beyond the "specialized" scientific beginnings he made, and he echoed arguments Ransom made in *I'll Take My Stand* with a commitment to them we found tenuous in Ransom. Ours, said Percy, is the age of the Theorist-Consumer—the theorist being that scientific specialist whose emphasis has been upon technological advances suited to consumerism. Both positions are less than adequate in Percy's estimate to the spiritual nature of man. One is reminded again of a remark by an admiring close friend of both Flannery O'Connor and Walker Percy, Professor Thomas Stritch of the University of Notre Dame, made in his recent *My Notre Dame: Memories and Reflections of Sixty Years*. Professor Stritch was also a lifelong familiar of and friend of the principal Agrarians, especially of Donald Davidson and Allen Tate. Those "Nashville thinkers," he recalled, "attacked, not so much the actual machinery of industrialism, but the kind of materialistic thinking machinery induced and faith in its unlimited progress and reason as the ultimate solver of all the ills of the world." Such, too, was Percy's position, as it was Flannery O'Connor's. Miss O'Connor, however, found Tate and Davidson and Lytle, as she found *I'll Take My Stand*, supportive of her own Thomistic position. Professor Stritch said to this point, reflecting on his own understanding of the Agrarians, "my Catholicism added a new dimension to my sympathy with agrarian ideals." He remembered as well that "Donald Davidson ... never became a formal [Catholic but was] deeply sympathetic to Catholic ideals." In that train of thought he concluded, "As I came to know Flannery O'Connor I began to see Catholicism a little as she did, as all or nothing.... In Flannery my southern-ness, my agrarian connections, and my Catholicism all merged."

My own point is that Percy might have concluded the same, had he looked more closely at the position. That he was sympathetic to Tate in particular is evident in his letters. One suspects he may have been cautious about the Agrarians because of the short-lived association they had with that strange editor of *The American Review*, Seward Collins, an association which has colored the popular academic view of the Agrarians ever since. The Agrarians broke relations with Collins, but without a sufficient acknowledgment of their rejection of Collins to their antagonists in the interval since the mid–1930s. Those anti–Agrarians on this score were less than honest in their tarring the Agrarians with Collins's Nazi sympathies.

As for Collins and *The American Review*, his first issue (April 1933) proposed in his "Editorial Notes" to bring together the Agrarians, the Neo-Thomists, the Chestertonian Distributists, and the Babbitt Humanists. That first issue does so rather impressively. There are essays by Hilaire Belloc, Christopher Dawson, and G. K. Chesterton. The Agrarian John Donald Wade (founding editor of the *Georgia Review*) has an essay on Joel Chandler Harris. Davidson reviews Arthur Schlesinger's *Rise of the City*. Paul Elmer More contributes a long essay on Marcel Proust. The next issue carries a continuation of Belloc's essay and Tate's satirical address to unemployment, "A Modest Proposal." There is also Ransom's famous essay on Milton's "Lycidas," "A Poem Almost Anonymous."

But Collins as a liability soon emerged in his pro–Nazi stance. Tate wrote Davidson (February 23, 1936): "[W]e've got to do something about Collins.... However valiant he has been in the cause, we can't let him make us Fascists when the big plank in our platform is that we are offering the sole alternative to Fascism." The Agrarians broke decisively with him, answering Collins's pro-fascist argument "I Want a King" in a piece dissociating the Agrarians from *The American Review*. Their "Fascism and the Southern Agrarians" appeared, not in the *American Review*, but in *The New Republic* in 1936. Collins had given them a forum for a time, but that association with the *American Review* had proved a continuing burden to their position in the subsequent intellectual rough and tumble where truth is not always so inviting an end as the repudiation of an antagonist. The same address to victory at all costs one might note in the contemporary adulation of a decided Nazi, now heralded by what purports to be democratic liberalism: the elevation of Margaret Sanger as the founder of Planned Parenthood. One is reminded of the parallel of Percy's fierce antagonism to abortion as championed by Sanger's disciples.

Margaret Sanger, in this era, is for the pro-abortion activists their version of Mother Teresa. But one finds them little aware of, or reluctant to face, the nature of her concern for abortion as a means of population control. As Robert Marshall and Charles Donovan show in their recent *Blessed Are the Barren: The Social Policy of Planned Parenthood* (Ignatius, 1992), Sanger was dominantly concerned with "the unbalance between the birth rate of the 'unfit' and the 'fit.'" This, she says, is "the greatest menace to civilization." Thus abortion becomes a necessary instrument of control, if America is to prevent being overrun by the blacks and by the "little brown people" who have "no traditions of democracy." Indeed, Sanger's sense of "democracy" is so closely paralleled to that sense of democracy advocated by the Third Reich as to make it quite clear that she is cheek by jowl with Hitlerian purifications of the populace, through eugenics as a program requiring abortion and, inescapably, euthanasia. One sees from this current veneration of Planned Parenthood and its founder Margaret Sanger just how appropriate Walker Percy's ironic words, in that interview for *Crisis* (September 1990): Our age of "the theorist-consumer" is "the most scientifically advanced, savage, democratic, inhuman, sentimental, murderous century in human history." He added, "Americans are the nicest, most generous and sentimental people on earth. Yet Americans have killed more unborn children than any nation in history. Now euthanasia is beginning."

We conclude, then, that we are still very much engaged in that struggle against modernist dislocations of intellect which the Agrarians and Distributists contended with, dislocations now settled from the regions of economics to the life of the family as the unit in social community. We must persevere in that continuing war, whose desirable end is a recovery of intellect to its unity so that it may recover its proper role as steward of being rather than dictator of being. We must recover certain realities distorted by idealist deconstructions of reality that have eroded community by destroying our understanding of the person as a created being responsible to an accommodation of history and nature through intellectual understanding. Knowledge as a possession of intuitive and rational intellect is the first recognition necessary to the recovery of personhood, after which follows the slow and difficult recovery of a community of intellect concerned to recover community itself from that divisiveness which makes it at once the most scientifically advanced and most savage, the most democratic and most inhuman, the most sentimental and most murderous community in the long history of mankind.

Notes

1. See *A Look at "The End of History?"* edited by Kenneth M. Jensen. Washington, D.C.: The United States Institute of Peace, 1990. See also Fukuyama's extension of his argument in his *The End of History and the Last Man*. New York: The Free Press, 1992.

2. It is over the question of faith that Voegelin and Leo Strauss reach a sort of parting of the ways in their relationship, in large part I suggest because a sufficient meaning of the term is not established between them. The issue emerges in their correspondence. See their letters and see also the essay in the same volume by Ellis Sandoz, "Medieval Rationalism or Mystic Philosophy? Reflections on the Strauss-Voegelin Correspondence," in *Faith and Political Philosophy*," edited by Peter Emberly and Barry Cooper, Pennsylvania State University Press, 1992. As for their relation as philosophical historians: history elevated to a secular science called historiography very much troubles both. Strauss in his Walgreen Lectures, *Natural Right and History*, explores the rise of historiography out of 18th century rationalism. Voegelin takes a longer view, from Joachim of Flora in the 12th century through Hegel to Marx, in his *Science, Politics & Gnosticism*, and in his own Walgreen Lectures, *The New Science of Politics*, analyzing the destructive consequences in the interest of our recovering a viable political philosophy. This latter work has increasingly commanded the attention of our academic "political scientists" over the past two decades, and with a gradual salutary effect.

3. With a little time and wit, one could develop parallels between late medieval scholasticism and modern economic scholasticism. Indeed, there is suggestive analogy between, say, such minds as that of the Father of Nominalism, William of Occam, and certain nominalists committed to the "index of Leading Indicators," to the intricate involvement, by definition, among such categories as *unemployment claims, building permits, unfilled orders for durables, money supply, stock prices, consumer confidence,* and

so on. The refining within the separate indicators is a challenge to scholastic ingenuity, as for instance the proposal regarding money supply of the importance of distinctions between "M-l," "M-2," and "M-3"—i.e., currency in circulation, savings accounts and mutual funds, and time deposits (Treasury bills, savings bonds, commercial paper and the like). One might, in such a playful mood, even find analogy between these dimensions of abstract accounting of material reality and the many species of grace in scholastic philosophy. Little wonder, given the indefinite intricacies of category, that a college of economic cardinals, roughly encompassing Washington, D.C., and supported by monastics in academic institutions, make daily assessments of the effects of these "graces" on the material well-being of the polity.

4. In June of 1992 at Palo Alto occurred the Third International Symposium on the History of Particle Physics (*Science News*, September 12, 1992). At that gathering some hundred physicists, philosophers and historians of particle physics gathered for accounts by leading particle physicists themselves of their participation in establishing the present formulation of the quark hypothesis, now the standard model for the discipline. A significant theme at the gathering is the relation of the theorist to the experimenter; another is the role of "luck" in the progress toward general acceptance of the model. At this point in the special knowing of the surface of reality which is designated particle physics, most of the physicists accept an objective reality as the challenge to their fuller understanding. The progress, said Steven Weinberg (University of Texas at Austin), "resembles climbing a peak.... There are many paths to the top. What makes the climb difficult on the disparate paths is the tension between the desire in the separate climber to achieve the peak and the resistance in the terrain of complex, objective reality itself." That terrain, separate from the climber and his intentionality, is the subject of the gathering's reminiscences of their journeying as particle physicists. Objective reality athwart intellectual desire, with occasional good "luck," affords some sense of a progress toward understanding. Michael Redhead, professor of the history and philosophy of science at the University of Cambridge, puts the tensional aspect succinctly: "We can always conjecture, but there is some control. The world [objective reality] kicks back."

5. I have spoken to the importance of St. Thomas' "principle of proper proportionality" in other works, and cite here the use I make of it in the Lamar Lectures, *Possum, and Other Receits for the Recovery of "Southern" Being*. It is through a pursuit of this principle by the rational intellect that one gains some glimpse of the mystery of the relation of the created

to the Creator. The argument, put in a simplified summary in the lectures, is as follows:

Being, the perfection of all perfections, cannot be conceptualized, as can *esse*. It is approached after conceptualization of *esse* occurs by the mind through a movement of mind—an act of judgment; what I suggest as an active assent. In this movement of mind from *esse* toward Being, mind is turned from itself and its own acts of conceptualizations outward to what is not itself and so on toward that which is ultimate, i.e. beyond conceptualization. The distinction of these two movements of mind (conceptualization and judgment) has its cause implicit in the formulation, "God *is esse*; creatures (*ens*) *have esse* but *are not esse*." Being may thus be recognized as an uncaused action beyond finite conceptualization. Hence it is called "the perfection of all perfections," the perfection whereby *beings* (*ens*) are. St. Augustine in retrospect acts out this movement of mind for us in his "Vision at Ostia" (Book 9, Chap. 10 of *The Confessions*). Following him, I suggest we already in a sense "know" this perfection through *intellectus*, as opposed to the knowing of the *ratio*, the conceptualizing agency of mind. That intuitive knowledge is already in the infant's clasp of its mother. Here is the movement in the visionary "confusion," a *fusion* of intuitive and rational intellect. That is the moment at which we are returned to known but forgotten things more fundamental than the limits of time and space. St. Augustine explores this movement at length and with wonder in Book 10 of *The Confessions*, "A Philosophy of Memory," and in Book 11, "Time and Eternity."

6. I have in mind once more not only Fukuyama's initiating essay, "The End of History," but his subsequent elaboration following the excited attention to the essay, *The End of History and the Last Man*, The Free Press, 1992.

7. For this reason, one might turn with profit to an incisive attempt to rescue the question of natural law to its proper grounding in reality: Russell Hittinger's "Natural Law in the Positive Laws: A Legislative or Adjudicative Issue?" *Review of Politics*, in press, is a healthful point of departure.

8. In my extended essay on John Stewart's *Burden of Time*, his massive and unsatisfactory engagement of the Fugitive-Agrarian phenomenon, I have explicated at length Ransom's "Bells for John Whiteside's Daughter" as a remarkable instance of classic drama written small. See my "Bells for John Stewart's Burden," *Georgia Review*, Summer 1966.

9. Mr. Ransom's attitude toward Agrarianism must be said, at the least, to have fluctuated. I have a letter from him (September 28, 1965) in

response to an earlier one of mine, following his visit to read at the University of Georgia. In part he said, "You ask me about the state of my Agrariansim at present.... My sense of the good life hasn't changed a bit. But, going frequently to Nashville, I've been extremely set back by the industrialization of that town which was once quiet, staid, and lovely.... I lead my own life better on this quiet Hill at Gambier, where I am in good company and pay almost no attention to the plains below." (One remembers, in a manner Tate might adapt, Heidegger on his mountain.) He then recalls his attempt to interest some students at Vanderbilt to do "what the Yankee Sherwood Anderson had done: he bought a country paper in the Shenandoah Valley" to make it "an organ for the county, not the county seat, with a touch of literature (the Bible, or something of his own composition) in every issue; and trying to recover the real life of the country community." The South, Ransom feared, "will become more and more like the North. But I take comfort in feeling that after all a man, and a family, can lead their own lives; we do, in my family." And he has added in script to the typed letter: "I run a garden, rather bigger than I can well manage." Some ten years later, when I wrote my Fugitive, I got his permission to use the letter as if addressed to my protagonist, who is intent on recovering himself and a county community. I hope the device amused Mr. Ransom.

10. Gilson, in his Methodical Realism (Christendom College Press, 1990), poses Thomistic "methodical realism" against the Cartesian idealism that has dominated Western thought since Decartes. Among his observations, explicated in some detail in these collected essays: "He who begins with Descartes, cannot avoid ending up with Berkeley or with Kant." Further, "Descartes, Kant, Comte all witness to the powerlessness of idealism to pass from criticism to positive construction." And again, "If one regards Cartesianism as a metaphysics, it ends in Berkeley's idealism; but when one regards it as a purely methodical idealism, it results in the critical idealism of Kant."

11. Ransom's objections were very early, but they followed the poem through its 70-year critical endurances of the criticism at other hands. I engage the question of the unity of the poem by arguing that the body of Eliot's poetry constitutes a sort of comedy possible to the modern poet whose intellectual journeying is like Dante's. What is denied the modern poet is the formal conveniences Dante enjoyed. Dante's poet, having arrived at and known the end of his journeying, begins in a mock innocence, as if the journey as he begins the composition of his great poem were just getting underway as the words are spoken. The formal structure

is assured thereby. In my comparative approach to *The Waste Land*, Eliot's poem becomes analogous to Dante's portion dramatizing the level of lower Hell, from which the protagonist Dante emerges onto Mt. Purgatory. But the maker of Dante's *Hell* has already experienced intellectually the "multifaliate rose" of that final ascent to the border of *Paradise*. The history of our intellectual fragmentation since the 13th century affords Eliot no such orderly address. See for this argument my *T. S. Eliot: An Essay on the American Magus* (1970) and my extended consideration of *The Waste Land* manuscript, *Eliot's Reflective Journey to the Garden* (1979).

12. A minor possible addition to Weaver's observation is in order; there is a formidable 3-volume study by Richard Beale Davis, *Intellectual Life in the Colonial South: 1585–1763* (Knoxville: University of Tennessee Press, 1978) which shows St. Thomas not foreign to Southern libraries, though of course he is, as Weaver says, no immediate influence on the generally inarticulate and little-read population. Weaver concludes that the Southerner "felt that a religion that is intellectual only is no religion."

13. In 1923, Ransom reviewed *The Waste Land* for the *Literary Review*, finding it chaotic as we have said, especially in respect to form. Eliot "is trying for novelty." But there "is not a single occasion where his context is as mature as the quotation which he inserts into it." It is one of those poems destined for rejection, since it is "subordinate" and "unequal," even to such a poem as "Prufrock." Tate responded in a fury to the *Literary Review* piece, sending a copy of his response to Ransom, who responded testily. Tate intended to have nothing more to do with Ransom from that point (1923), but Davidson managed to smooth the waters between them. We should note carefully that this tensional relation would continue. It is in that letter of Tate's to Davidson in 1952, though we notice as well that by that late date Ransom no longer would pronounce *The Waste Land* a critical reject. At Eliot's death, Tate edited a special issue of the *Sewanee Review*, to which Ransom was invited to contribute. It seems characteristic, in retrospect, that Ransom's piece was not ready for the issue and was published separately later, though included in the book version of the tributes. It seems of some interest as well that Ransom chose to write on "Gerontion," rather than on *The Waste Land* or any of Eliot's subsequent poetry.

14. In the year after Tate entered the Church, Jacques and Raissa Maritain worked at their translation of Tate's "Ode to the Confederate Dead," and Tate corresponded with them, enthusiastic about their progress. He wrote Raissa (November 28, 1951) about the general project and remarks specifically on the phrase *more hopeful*: "There is a single word

that I might question, but I do not know enough [French] to question it with conviction. I refer to *optimistes*....

> Shall we, more hopeful,
> Set up the grave in the house?

'More hopeful' has some of the connotation of Hope, the theological virtue, rather than of optimism as opposed to pessimism. What I am saying, I suppose, is that in this passage Christian Hope, based upon Faith in the after-life, is ironically perverted into a cult of death." Raissa substitutes "*Avec plus d'esperance*," which Tate finds (December 14, 1951) "renders exactly the intentions of *more hopeful*." See these letters in *Exiles and Fugitives: The Letters of Jacques and Raissa Maritain, Allen Tate, and Caroline Gordon*, edited by John M. Dunaway, Louisiana State University Press, 1992.

15. Richard Weaver would no doubt reject such a claim, himself so resolutely Protestant by tradition. It is evident from a brief note to me from Tate that the two were less personally compatible than, say, Weaver with Davidson. I had sent Tate my "Richard Weaver against the Establishment," and he wrote (January 25, 1970), "I suppose I never admired Weaver as much as he deserved. I did admire his stance and his courage, but I thought his Thomism a little shallow." At the heart of this incompatibility, rather surely, is the distance between Tate, then a Roman, and Weaver, still very intimately a part of the Weaver family's Protestant tradition, centered in Weaverville, North Carolina, which was always home to Richard Weaver though he was long resident in Chicago.

Index

Aeneid 92
Ages of Gaia: A Biography of the Living Earth (Lovelock) 50, 52
Aiken, Conrad 12
Allen Tate: A Literary Biography (Squires) 100
American Quarterly 95
The American Review 140
Aristotle 134
Art and Scholasticism (Maritain) 104, 105
Atlanta Constitution 73
Auden, W. H. 12

Barr, Stringfellow 80
Barrett, William 12
Belloc, Hilaire 140
Bergson, Henri 51
Between Nothingness and Paradise (Niemeyer) 69
Blessed Are the Barren: The Social Policy of Planned Parenthood (Donovan and Marshall) 141
Bohr, Niels 25
Bork, Robert 65
Brooks, Cleanth 85, 95
Brother to Dragons (Warren) 94
Brown, John 128
Burden of Time: The Fugitives and Agrarians (Stewart) 11
Burke, Kenneth 85

Chesterton, G. K. 26, 68, 69, 83, 84, 98, 140; *The Everlasting Man* 68; *Orthodoxy* 68

Collins, Seward 140ff
Comte, Auguste 69
Creative Intuition and Poetic Knowledge (Maritain) 104–5
Crisis 139, 141

Dante 11, 12, 92–93; *Divine Comedy*, 92, 93, 95, 123
Davidson, Donald: *Attack on Leviathan: Regionalism and Nationalism in the United States*, 128; "On a Replica of the Parthenon" 132; *The Tall Men* 131
Dawson, Christopher 140
Descartes, René 81, 109
Distributists 22, 26, 27, 98, 126, 142
Donne, John 53
Donovan, Charles 141
Dryden, John 128

Eliot, T. S. *After Strange Gods: A Primer of Modern Heresy* 106, 137, 138; "Ash-Wednesday" 131; *Collected Poems: 1909-1962* 130; "The Metaphysical Poets" 127; "The Modern Mind" 105; "The Perfect Critic" 104; "The Pseudo-Determinists' Ideas of Economics" 137; "Tradition and the Individual Talent" 102, 104, 137; *The Uses of Poetry and the Uses of Criticism* 105; *The Waste Land* 13, 82, 85–86, 102–6, 108, 124, 131
Ethics of Rhetoric (Weaver) 30
The Everlasting Man (Chesterton) 68, 69

Index

"Fascism and the Southern Agrarians" 141
Faulkner, William 75
Fitzgerald, F. Scott 77
Fitzgerald, Robert 138
Frost, Robert 51
The Fugitive 139
Fukuyama, Francis, 19, 61

Gentleman in a Dustcoat (Young) 87
Georgia Review 140
Gilson, Etienne 81, 82, 97, 123, 137

Harris, Joel Chandler 140
Hegel 54, 73
Hemingway, Ernest 77
Hitler, Adolph 60, 78, 126
Homer 77
Hopkins, Gerard Manley 49
Hugh Selwyn Mauberley (Pound) 77
Humanists 126
Hunter, Gordon 95–96

"I Want a King" 141
Ideas Have Consequences (Weaver) 30, 122
I'll Take My Stand 54, 66, 87, 93, 98, 108, 112, 122, 123, 129, 131, 137, 139, 140; "Statement of Principles" 66, 73, 80, 88, 127

Jackson, Stonewall 128
Jefferson, Thomas 90
John Wesley (Wade) 128
Joyce, James 91
Julian of Norwich 47, 49

Kant, Immanuel 81, 84, 87, 97, 109
Keats, John 35, 93
Kenyon Review 82, 88, 89, 95, 96, 134

Lewis, C. S. 137
Literary Review 13
Locke, John 133
Lovelock, James 52
Lowell, Robert 12, 138
Lytle, Andrew 11, 84, 86, 88, 97, 128,

139; *Bedford Forrest and His Critter Company* 128

Marcel, Gabriel 137
Maritain, Jacques 79, 86, 99, 101, 104ff, 109, 130, 137; *Art and Scholasticism* 104, 105; *Creative Intuition and Poetic Knowledge* 104, 105
Maritain, Raissa 79, 99, 109
Marshall, John 114ff
Marshall, Robert 141
Marx, Karl 54, 75
McGill, Ralph 73
Metaphysics of Language (Parain) 33
Milton, John 128, 134
Mims, Edwin 95
More, Paul Elmer 140
Mother Teresa 141
My Notre Dame: Memories and Reflections of Sixty Years (Stritch) 139

New Republic 130, 141
Niemeyer, Gerhart 69, 137

O'Connor, Flannery 76, 138, 139, 140
"Ode to a Nightingale" (Keats) 35
O'Donnell, George Marion 91
Odyssey 92
"The Older Religiousness of the South" (Weaver) 122
Orthodoxy (Chesterton) 68
"Ozymandias" (Shelley) 24

Parain, Brice 33
Partisan Review 12, 13
Pascal, Blaise 123, 124
Pensées 124
Percy, Walker 76, 138ff
Pisan Cantos (Pound) 12, 93
Plato 20
Poetry Magazine 100
Porter, Katherine Anne 12
A Portrait of the Artist as a Young Man (Joyce) 91–92
Pound, Ezra 12, 51, 77, 93, 127; *Hugh Selwyn Mauberley* 77; *Pisan Cantos* 12, 93

Index

Ransom, John Crowe: "Bells for John Whiteside's Daughter" 12, 134; "Captain Carpenter" 127, 134; "The Concrete Universal" 88; *God without Thunder* 87; "Piazza Piece" 87; "A Poem Almost Anonymous" 140; "Reconstructed but Unregenerate" 80, 83, 88, 108; "Theory of Poetic Form" 85; "What Does the South Want" 79, 88, 90; *The World's Body* 89, 97, 128
"The Religious Poetry of Robert Penn Warren" (Southard) 96
"Retrospective: Reviewing America: John Crowe Ransom's *Kenyon Review*" (Hunter) 95
Rise of the City (Schlesinger) 140
Robespierre 48, 51
Roosevelt, Franklin Delano 90

Sanger, Margaret 141
Schlesinger, Arthur 140
Science, Politics & Gnosticism (Voegelin) 72
Shapiro, Karl 12
Shelley, Percy Bysshe 24
Siger de Brabant 15
Solzhenitsyn, Alexander 61
Southard, W. P. 96
Squires, Radcliffe 100
Stalin, Josef 60, 126
"Statement of Principles" 66, 73, 80, 88, 127
Stevens, Wallace 87, 100ff
Stevenson, Adlai 101
Stewart, John L. 11, 13
Stritch, Thomas 139
"Sunday Morning" (Stevens) 100
Symposium on Formalist Criticism (Burke, ed.) 85

Tate, Allen: "A Modest Proposal," 140; "The New Provincialism" 78–79; "Notes on Liberty and Property" 111; "Ode to the Confederate Dead" 102, 109, 131; "Remarks on the Southern Religion" 122
"Things of August" (Stevens) 100, 109
Thomas Aquinas, St. 15, 26, 39, 40, 45, 57, 62–63, 86; *On Being and Essence* 57; *On the Unity of the Intellect Against the Averroists* 129; *Summa Theologica* 57, 129, 139
Thomas, Clarence 65
Tolkien, J. R. R. 137
"Tracts Against Communism" (Warren) 54, 73

Virgil 11, 77
Voegelin, Eric 20, 25, 60, 72, 83, 98, 116, 137, 143; *Science, Politics & Gnosticism* 72

Wade, John Donald 128, 140
Warren, Robert Penn 11, 12, 86, 90, 94, 96, 98, 128; "Tracts Against Communism" 54, 73
Weaver, Richard 30, 122, 125, 129
Who Owns America: A New Declaration of Independence (Agar and Tate) 22, 27, 79, 80, 85, 88, 98, 110, 111
Wordsworth, William 35, 37
Works and Days (Hesiod) 92

You, Emperors, and Others: Poems 1957-1960 (Warren) 94
Young, Daniel 87, 96
Young, Stark 125

www.ingramcontent.com/pod-product-compliance
Lightning Source LLC
Chambersburg PA
CBHW032105300426
44116CB00007B/895